ሰዋስው
TIGRINYA GRAMMAR

Edited by
John Mason

The Red Sea Press, Inc.
Publishers & Distributors of Third World Books
11-D Princess Road
Lawrenceville, NJ 08648

The Red Sea Press, Inc.
11 Princess Road, Suite D
Lawrenceville, New Jersey 08648

©1994, 1996, American Evangelical Mission

First Red Sea Press, Inc., Edition 1996

All rights reserved. No parts of this publication may
be reproduced, stored in a retrieval system or transmitted
in any form or by any means electronic, mechanical,
photocopying, recording or otherwise without the prior
written permission of the publisher.

Cover Design: Linda Nickens

Library of Congress Cataloging-in-Publication Data:

Tigrinya grammar / edited by John Mason.
    p.   cm.
  English and Tigrinya.
  ISBN 0-932415-20-2. -- ISBN 0-932415-21-0 (pbk.)
  1. Tigrinya language--Grammar.   I. Mason, John S., 1945-
PJ9111.T54 1996
492'.8--dc20   95-26821
                                                            CIP

CONTENTS

Introduction iv
Part I Tigrinya and its Alphabets 1
Part II Lessons 8
1 What is This? With Replies 8
2 What are These?
    What are Those? 11
3 Adjectives 14
4 Plurals of Adjectives 15
5 Demonstrative Adjectives 17
6 The Verb "to be" and
    Subjective Pronouns 19
7 Negative of the Verb "to be" 21
8 "Give me" and "Show me" .. 22
9 Cardinal Numbers 23
10 The Calendar 25
11 Telling Time 27
12 Present Tense of
    "to be present" 29
13 Common Prepositions 31
14 Compound Prepositions 33
15 Pronominal Suffixes 34
16 Possessive Pronouns 36
17 The Verb 37
18 Simple Perfect of
    All Verb Families 44
19 Simple Imperfect of
    All Verb Families 47
20 Gerundive 50
21 Gerundive in Subordinate
    Clauses 51
22 Imperative-Jussive 52
23 Future Tense 53
24 Negative of All Tenses 54
25 Infinitives, Adverbial and
    Nounal 55

26 The Verb "to have" 56
27 Negative of the Verb
    "to have" 58
28 Object Suffixes in
    Simple Perfect 59
29 More Prepositions and
    Pronoun Objects 65
30 Adverbs 67
31 Compound Tenses,
    ነበረ and ኮይኑ 73
32 Verbal Adjectives and
    Nouns 76
33 Ordinal Numbers 78
34 Direct and Indirect Objects ... 79
35 Interogatives 82
36 Causatives 84
37 Passives 86
38 Relatives 88
39 Comparatives and
    Superlatives 92
40 Coordinate Conjunctions
    and Interjections 93
41 Subordinate Conjuctions 98
42 Reciprocals and
    Frequentatives 102
43 በል Verb 104
44 Direct Speech 107
45 Indirect Discourse 109
46 Defective and Irregular
    Verbs 112
47 Impersonal Verbs 115
48 Stative Tenses 117
49 Conditionals 118

Part III Common Expressions ... 121

Introduction

This short handbook of the Tigrinya language is for anyone speaking English who wants to study Tigrinya. It has been derived from language learning materials prepared by the Inter-Mission Language Council in 1968. These materials were distributed in mimeograph form. However, the development of the computer and especially desktop publishing has made it possible to republish the grammar with a more legible typeface. The Orthodox Presbyterian Church was interested in the project and helped materially with it. The process of typesetting the work gave the opportunity to do editing of content as well.

I am grateful to Kibrom Tseggai for his help on many aspects of the book. The Tigrinya language is changing continually. Although the examples and rules given here are as far as possible normal, correct usage, this is a descriptive grammar, not a prescriptive one.

The grammar includes a list of common phrases. Those who want to learn spoken Tigrinya should memorize such expressions early on. This will open the door for conversation and practice.

The revision of this grammar has been accompanied by prayers that it will be useful for the enjoyment of liberty in Eritrea.

PART I

Tigrinya and its Alphabet

TIGRINYA is one of the designated national languages of Eritrea and is probably the language most widely spoken there. It belongs to a family of related languages that A. L. Schlözer named the "Semitic" languages (1781). This family includes notably Arabic and Hebrew, as well as Aramaic and other Near Eastern languages like Ugaritic, which is known only from inscriptions. Tigrinya shows clearly the characteristic features of a Semitic language. The most important is the verb system, which has two "tenses," but several "aspects" (causative, intensive, reflexive, etc.). Another feature is the apparent derivation of related words from "roots" consisting of three consonants. For instance, ጸሓፊ *secretary;* መጽሓፍ *book;* ጸሓፈ *he wrote.*

Tigrinya uses a special writing system called the "Ge'ez" (or "Ethiopic") alphabet (or syllabary). The earliest inscription in Ge'ez is without vowels. However, at some point in the distant past, the vowels of the language began to be written by way of small additions or modifications to the consonants preceding them. Thus, although Arabic and Hebrew are usually written without vowels (or "unpointed"), languages that use the Ge'ez alphabet are always vowelled.

The normal syllable in Tigrinya is considered to be a consonant followed by a vowel. If a consonant ends a syllable, the sixth, neutral vowel is used with it. Most consonants are written in seven slightly different forms corresponding to the traditional seven vowels. The next table shows the vowels, including their traditional names. The system of vowels applied to all the consonants is exhibited in the alphabet chart, commonly called "ha hu" after the first two letters.

name	order	sound	transliteration	example	
ገዐዝ	1st	ĕ as in d*e*n (or ă)	e (or a)	ሀ	ha/he
ካዕብ	2nd	ū as in l*u*te	u	ሁ	hu
ሣልስ	3rd	ē as in s*ea*	i	ሂ	hi
ራብዕ	4th	ă as in f*a*ther	a	ሃ	ha
ሓምስ	5th	ie as in V*ie*tnam	ie	ሄ	hie
ሳድስ	6th	(neutral or null)	(not fixed)	ህ	h
ሳብዕ	7th	ō as in v*o*te	o	ሆ	ho

The alphabet chart shows the Ge'ez letters including some that are rarely seen. The column of pronunciations is given as a help for using the chart and memorizing the letters. The actual sounds of the letters, not to mention how to read them in context, can only be learned from an informant.

The traditional sound of the first vowel is ĕ, but for a few letters the first vowel was sounded ă, the same as the 4th vowel. These exceptions were notably ሀ, ሐ, and አ. Recently in Eritrea, and in the field especially, the alphabet has been written in a more consistent way, so that in the 1st form these three characters are given the vowel ĕ ; like the other letters. This means that the letter አ is now being displaced by the 4th form ኣ in many words. The pronunciation of the words is the same in the old spelling and in the new. For example, አሎ and ኣሎ are the same word pronounced the same way, but the spelling with አ is preferred.

The letters as normally printed conform closely to those produced in handwriting done by scribes with calligraphic pens that vary the width of the strokes according to their direction. Vertical strokes are wide and horizontal ones are narrow. Handwriting done with other pens or pencils does not reproduce this feature and is not standardized.

Typewritten letters can be difficult to read, and a table of these forms is included for help on that point.

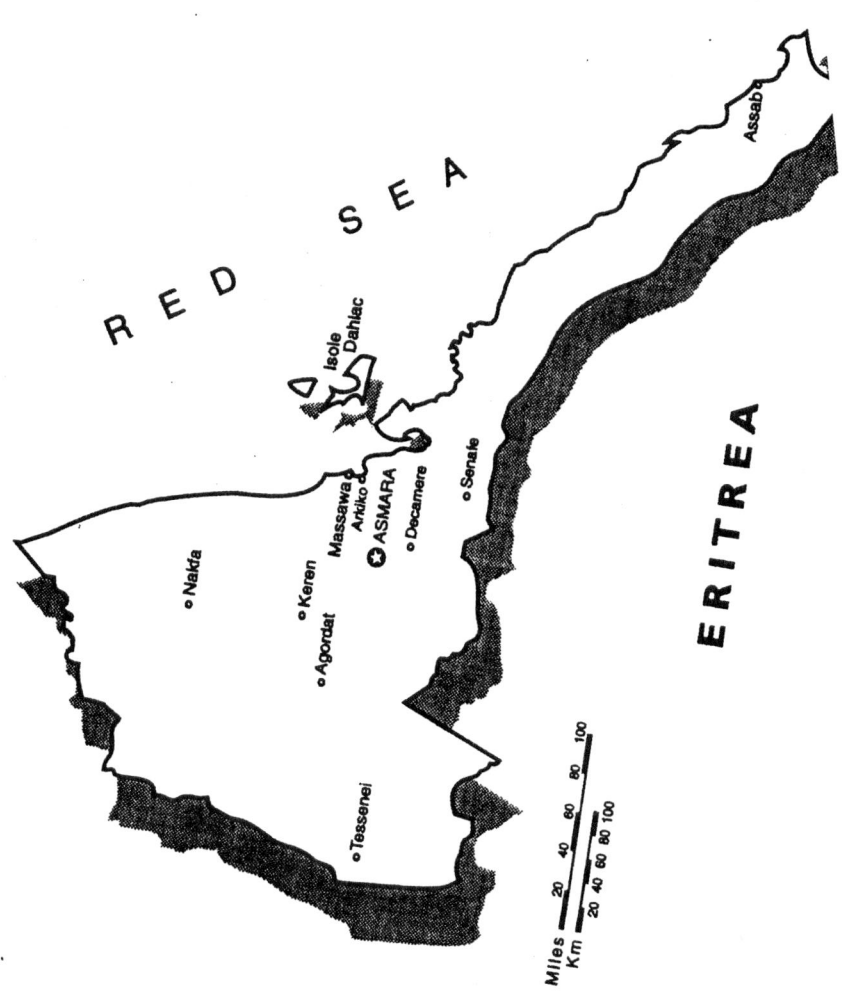

The Tigrinya Alphabet

ሀ	ሁ	ሂ	ሃ	ሄ	ህ	ሆ	h
ለ	ሉ	ሊ	ላ	ሌ	ል	ሎ	l
ሐ	ሑ	ሒ	ሓ	ሔ	ሕ	ሖ	ḥ pharyngeal
መ	ሙ	ሚ	ማ	ሜ	ም	ሞ	m
ሠ	ሡ	ሢ	ሣ	ሤ	ሥ	ሦ	s old style
ረ	ሩ	ሪ	ራ	ሬ	ር	ሮ	r
ሰ	ሱ	ሲ	ሳ	ሴ	ስ	ሶ	s
ሸ	ሹ	ሺ	ሻ	ሼ	ሽ	ሾ	sh
ቀ	ቁ	ቂ	ቃ	ቄ	ቅ	ቆ	q
ቐ	ቑ	ቒ	ቓ	ቔ	ቕ	ቖ	q laryngeal
በ	ቡ	ቢ	ባ	ቤ	ብ	ቦ	b
ተ	ቱ	ቲ	ታ	ቴ	ት	ቶ	t
ቸ	ቹ	ቺ	ቻ	ቼ	ች	ቾ	ch
ኀ	ኁ	ኂ	ኃ	ኄ	ኅ	ኆ	h
ነ	ኑ	ኒ	ና	ኔ	ን	ኖ	n
ኘ	ኙ	ኚ	ኛ	ኜ	ኝ	ኞ	ñ
አ	ኡ	ኢ	ኣ	ኤ	እ	ኦ	' glottal stop
ከ	ኩ	ኪ	ካ	ኬ	ክ	ኮ	k
ኸ	ኹ	ኺ	ኻ	ኼ	ኽ	ኾ	ch lo*ch*
ወ	ዉ	ዊ	ዋ	ዌ	ው	ዎ	w
ዐ	ዑ	ዒ	ዓ	ዔ	ዕ	ዖ	' Ar. ayin
ዘ	ዙ	ዚ	ዛ	ዜ	ዝ	ዞ	z
ዠ	ዡ	ዢ	ዣ	ዤ	ዥ	ዦ	zh azure
የ	ዩ	ዪ	ያ	ዬ	ይ	ዮ	y
ደ	ዱ	ዲ	ዳ	ዴ	ድ	ዶ	d
ጀ	ጁ	ጂ	ጃ	ጄ	ጅ	ጆ	j
ገ	ጉ	ጊ	ጋ	ጌ	ግ	ጎ	g

ጠ	ጡ	ጢ	ጣ	ጤ	ጥ	ጦ	ṭ plosive
ጨ	ጩ	ጪ	ጫ	ጬ	ጭ	ጮ	ch plosive
አ	ኡ	ኢ	ኣ	ኤ	እ	ኦ	p
ጸ	ጹ	ጺ	ጻ	ጼ	ጽ	ጾ	ts plosive
ፀ	ፁ	ፂ	ፃ	ፄ	ፅ	ፆ	ጸ old style
ፈ	ፉ	ፊ	ፋ	ፌ	ፍ	ፎ	f
ፐ	ፑ	ፒ	ፓ	ፔ	ፕ	ፖ	p
ቨ	ቩ	ቪ	ቫ	ቬ	ቭ	ቮ	v
ኰ		ኲ	ኳ	ኴ	ኵ		kʷ
ኾ		ዀ	ዂ	ዃ	ዅ		khʷ
ቈ		ቊ	ቋ	ቌ	ቍ		qʷ
ቘ		ቚ	ቛ	ቜ	ቝ		qʷ laryngeal
ጐ		ጒ	ጓ	ጔ	ጕ		gʷ
ኈ		ኊ	ኋ	ኌ	ኍ		hʷ

ኣ	ማ	ዘ	ቧ	ሿ	ቧ	other forms
ቷ	ቿ	ኗ	ኟ	ኻ	ዟ	
ዿ	ጧ	ጯ	ጿ	ፏ		

፩	፪	፫	፬	፭	፮	፯	፰	፱	፲	numerals
1	2	3	4	5	6	7	8	9	10	
፲	፳	፴	፵	፶	፷	፸	፹	፺	፻	
10	20	30	40	50	60	70	80	90	100	

፡ ፨ ፠ ፣ ፤ ፥   punctuation

ሀ	ሁ	ሂ	ሃ	ሄ	ህ	ሆ
ለ	ሉ	ሊ	ላ	ሌ	ል	ሎ
ሐ	ሑ	ሒ	ሓ	ሔ	ሕ	ሖ
መ	ሙ	ሚ	ማ	ሜ	ም	ሞ
ረ	ሩ	ሪ	ራ	ሬ	ር	ሮ
ሰ	ሱ	ሲ	ሳ	ሴ	ስ	ሶ
ሸ	ሹ	ሺ	ሻ	ሼ	ሽ	ሾ
ቀ	ቁ	ቂ	ቃ	ቄ	ቅ	ቆ
ቐ	ቑ	ቒ	ቓ	ቔ	ቕ	ቖ
በ	ቡ	ቢ	ባ	ቤ	ብ	ቦ
ተ	ቱ	ቲ	ታ	ቴ	ት	ቶ
ነ	ኑ	ኒ	ና	ኔ	ን	ኖ
ኘ	ኙ	ኚ	ኛ	ኜ	ኝ	ኞ
አ	ኡ	ኢ	ኣ	ኤ	እ	ኦ
ከ	ኩ	ኪ	ካ	ኬ	ክ	ኮ
ኸ	ኹ	ኺ	ኻ	ኼ	ኽ	ኾ
ወ	ዉ	ዊ	ዋ	ዌ	ው	ዎ
ዐ	ዑ	ዒ	ዓ	ዔ	ዕ	ዖ
ዘ	ዙ	ዚ	ዛ	ዜ	ዝ	ዞ
ዠ	ዡ	ዢ	ዣ	ዤ	ዥ	ዦ
የ	ዩ	ዪ	ያ	ዬ	ይ	ዮ
ደ	ዱ	ዲ	ዳ	ዴ	ድ	ዶ
ገ	ጉ	ጊ	ጋ	ጌ	ግ	ጎ

PART II

LESSON 1

What is this? with Replies

The normal word order in simple sentences is:
SUBJECT, OTHER PARTS, VERB.

እዚ መጽሓፍ እዩ። *This is a book.*

In simple questions, the normal order is:
DEMONSTRATIVE PRONOUN, INTERROGATIVE PRONOUN, VERB.

እዚ እንታይ እዩ፧ *What is this?*

(One also hears እንታይ እዩ እዚ፧) In the reply to the question, the demonstrative pronoun may be omitted.

እዚ እንታይ እዩ፧ መጽሓፍ እዩ። *What is this? It is a book.*

Most nouns in Tigrinya do not have special forms to distinguish masculine and feminine genders. There is no neuter form. Nouns are masculine or feminine by nature, e.g. ወዲ *boy* (m.), ጓል *girl* (f.), ሰብኣይ *man* (m.), ሰበይቲ *woman* (f.), ኣቦ *father* (m.), ኣደ *mother* (f.), ላም *cow* (f.); or by custom, e.g. ጸሓይ *sun* (f.), ወርሒ *moon* (f.), ቀንዴል or ሽምዓ *candle* (f.), ኩዕሶ *ball* (f.), ኮኾብ *star* (m.), ወረቐት *paper* (m.), ማዕጾ *door* (m.), ዘርኢ *seed* (m.), ንፋስ *wind* (m.). Some nouns, including most nouns describing inanimate objects, can be used in either gender, e.g. ገዛ *house*, ቤት *house*. But ቆልዓ *child* and ኣንበሳ *animal* have their gender according to the context.

The demonstrative pronouns are inflected for gender.

| እዚ | እዚኣ | this | (m., f.) |
| እቲ | እቲኣ | that | (m., f.) |

The corresponding polite forms are

| እዚኦም | እዚኤን | these persons | (m., f.) |
| እቲኦም | እቲኤን | those persons | (m., f.) |

In the 2nd and 3rd persons, the Tigrinya verb is inflected for gender as well as number. In other words, when the subject is "you," Tigrinya can use four different verb forms, depending on whether the "you" is a man, a woman, a group of men, or a group of women. In the same way, the third person subjects "he," "she," "they (men)," and "they (women)," will require different forms of the verb.

ንሱ ወዲ እዩ። *He is a boy.*
ንሳ ጓል እያ። *She is a girl.*
እቲ መስኮት እዩ። *That is a window.*
እቲኣ ኩዕሶ እያ። *That is a ball.*
ንስኺ ኣብዚ ኔርኪ። *You (a girl) were here.*
ንሳቶም ኣብ ከረን ነይሮም። *They (the men) were at Keren.*
ንሳተን ሎሚ ናብ ከተማ ከይደን። *Today they (the women) went to the city.*

Questions to be answered by "yes" or "no" make use of the suffix ዶ, affixed to the word which is emphasized. In addition, a rising tone is used.

እዚዶ መንበር እዩ፧ *Is this a chair?*

An affirmative answswer to such a question is indicated by **አወ**, which is invariant in form.

እዚዶ ብርዒ እዩ፤ አወ። *Is this a pen? Yes.*
እዚኣ ጓል ዲያ፤ አወ። *Is this a girl? Yes.*

A negative answer to such a question, however, requires a form of the verb **አይኮነን** *it is not*–agreeing with the subject.

እዚዶ መጽሓፍ እዩ፤ አይኮነን። *Is this a book? No, it isn't.*
እዚኣዶ ሽምዓ እያ፤ አይኮነትን። *Is this a candle? No.*

The noun may or may not be repeated in the negative reply.

LESSON 2

What are These? What are Those?

DEMONSTRATIVES

The demonstrative pronouns, **እኒ**, **እቲ**, have masculine and feminine forms in both singular and plural. In the spoken language, the polite forms of demonstratives and possessives are frequently used as plurals.

	Singular		Plural		Polite Forms
masc.	እኒ	this	እኒአቶም	these	እኒአም
fem.	እኒአ	this	እኒአተን	these	እኒኤን
masc.	እቲ	that	እቲአቶም	those	እቲአም
fem.	እቲአ	that	እቲአተን	those	እቲኤን

PLURALS OF NOUNS

1. Many nouns form their plural through the addition of a suffix. In the class of nouns whose plural can be formed by rule, those which add **ታት** are the most common.

    እምባ mountain, **እምባታት** mountains.

   (a) even here the **ታት** cannot be added without certain vowel changes. If the noun ends in 3rd form, e.g. **ክፍሊ** room, the last letter must be changed to 6th form before adding **ታት**.

    ክፍሊ room, **ክፍልታት** rooms

   (b) If the noun ends in 6th form, the last letter in most nouns changes to 4th form and adds only **ት**, e.g.

    ጥራዝ notebook, **ጥራዛት** notebooks

11

(c) Some plurals add the suffix ት but incorporate other changes as well, e.g.

ስም *name* ኣስማት *names*
ወዲ *boy* ኣወዳት *boys.*

2. Tigrinya is one of the South Semitic languages and has "internal" or "broken" plurals. These are plurals formed through changes inside the word rather than by suffixes. They may follow certain patterns, but often, while the resemblance between two plurals is apparent, it can hardly be reduced to a rule. Examples:

መንበር *chair,* መናብር *chairs*
ወኻርያ *fox,* ወኻሩ *foxes*
ገመል *camel,* ኣግማል *camels*
ላም *cow,* ኣሓ *cattle*
ሰብኣይ *man,* ሰብኡት *men*

3. Some nouns have two plural forms.

ጓል *girl,* ኣዋልድ or ኣንላት *girls*
መበለት *widow,* መበላሉ or መበላታት *widows.*

4. Plurals of inanimate objects are mostly treated as collective and usually take singular pronoun and verb.

እዚ መናብር እዩ። *These are chairs.*
እቲ ብርዕታት እዩ። *Those are pens.*

5. The forms of the negative *it is not* are:

	Singular		Plural	
masc.	ኣይኮነን	*it is not*	ኣይኮኑን	*they are not*
fem.	ኣይኮነትን	*it is not*	ኣይኮናን	*they are not*

እዚኣቶም አወዳት አይኮኑን። *These are not boys.*
እቲኣተን አዋልድ አይኮናን። *These are not girls.*

In some regions, when a noun is used with a numerical adjective, the noun may stay in the singular form although the verb is plural. But it is usual to have the plural of the noun also.

ክልተ ሰብአይ ናብ ቤተ መቕደስ ደየቡ። *Two men went up to the temple.*

ክልተ አሰብኡት ናብ ቤተ መቕደስ ደየቡ። *Two men went up to the temple.* (preferred usage)

13

LESSON 3

Adjectives

The adjective precedes the noun or pronoun which it modifies and agrees with it in gender and number.

ጽቡቅ ወዲ *handsome boy*
ጽብቅቲ ጓል *pretty girl*

1. Some adjectives form the feminine regularly.

   (a) Adjectives whose second-to-last letter is 2nd form change that letter to 6th form and add ቲ . (In the example ፉ has the 2d vowel and changes to ፍ , with the 6th vowel. Then the final ቲ is added.)

   ንፉዕ ንፍዕቲ *clever*

   (b) Adjectives whose second-to-last letter is 3rd form change that letter to 4th form.

   ሓጺር ሓጻር *short*

   (c) Adjectives whose second-to-last letter is 4th form in the masculine singular show no change for the feminine.

   ሓያል ሓያል *strong*
   ለባም ለባም *wise*

2. Some adjectives form the femine irregularly.

   ዓብዪ ዓባይ *great*
   ቀይሕ ቀያሕ *red*

14

LESSON 4

Plurals of Adjectives

Plurals of inanimate objects are often treated as collective and usually take a singular adjective and verb.

እቲ ጥራዛት ዓብዪ'ዶ እዩ፤   *Are these large notebooks?*
አይኮነን። ንእሽቶ እዩ።   *No, they are small.*

1. The plurals of some adjectives are formed regularly.

   (a) Adjectives whose next-to-last radical in the masculine singular is 2nd form change the final radical to 4th form and add ት.

   ንፉዕ   ንፉዓት   *clever*

   (b) Adjectives whose next-to-last radical in the masculine singular is 3rd form change the final radical to 1st form and add ቲ.

   ሓጺር   ሓጸርቲ   *short*
   ጸሊም   ጸለምቲ   *black*

   Adjectives in this class that end in ሕ are exceptions. These make the plural for both masculine and feminine by adding ቲ to the feminine singular. ("c." means "common" gender.)

   ነዊሕ (m.), ነዋሕ (f.), ነዋሕቲ (plural, c.)   *tall*
   ጸፊሕ (m.), ጸፋሕ (f.), ጸፋሕቲ (plural, c.)   *flat*

(c) As has been observed, adjectives whose second-to-last letter is 4th form in the masculine singular do not change for the feminine singular. These adjectives have a common plural also and it is made by changing the last radical to 4th form and adding ት.

ለባም ለባማት wise

2. The plurals of some adjectives are formed irregularly. And as with nouns, some adjectives have more than one plural.

ዓብይ (m.), ዓባይ (f.), ዓበይቲ (plural, c.) *great*

ንእሽቶ (sing, c.), ናእሽቱ (plural, c.) *small*

ዓሻ (sing, c.), ዓያሹ or ዓሻታት (plural, c.) *foolish*

LESSON 5

Demonstrative Adjectives

The demonstrative adjectives can be repeated and so have an initial and a secondary form.

እዚ ... እዚ	(m.s.) *this* (nearby objects)
እዛ ... እዚኣ	(f.s.) *this*
እዞም ... እዚኦም	(m.pl.) *these*
እዘን ... እዚኤን	(f.pl.) *these*
እቲ ... እቲ	(m.s.) *that* (remote objects)
እታ ... እቲኣ	(f.s.) *that*
እቶም ... እቲኦም	(m.pl.) *those*
እተን ... እቲኤን	(f.pl.) *those*

The noun comes between the two adjectives.

> እዚ ወዲ እዚ ንፉዕ እዩ። *This boy is clever.*
> እተን አንስቲ እቲኤን ኩናማ እየን። *Those women are Kunama.*

Less formally, the demonstrative adjective may not be repeated.

> እዚ ወዲ ንፉዕ እዩ። *This boy is clever.*
> እተን አንስቲ ኩናማ እየን። *Those women are Kunama.*

Note that the demonstrative adjectives are identical in form with the demonstrative pronouns. The following examples illustrate the differences in syntax.

እዚ ጽቡቕ ገዛ እዚ ናተይ እዩ።
(adj.) *This beautiful house is mine.*

እዚ ጽቡቕ ገዛ እዩ።
(pron.) *This is a beautiful house.*

እዚ መንበር እዚ ድልዱል እዩ።
(adj.) *This chair is strong.*

እዚ ድልዱል መንበር እዩ።
(pron.) *This is a strong chair.*

እዚ መንበር እዚ ናተይ ኣይኮነን።
(adj.) *This chair is not mine.*

እዚ መንበር ኣይኮነን።
(pron.) *This is not a chair.*

LESSON 6

The Verb "to be" and Subject Pronouns

The verb "to be" in the present tense is conjugated as follows. (Some writers use አ instead of ኢ in some forms.)

	Singular		Plural	
3 m.	ኢዩ	he is	ኢዮም	they are
f.	ኢያ	she is	ኢየን	they are
2 m.	ኢኻ	you are	ኢኹም	you are
f.	ኢኺ	you are	ኢኽን	you are
1 c.	እየ	I am	ኢና	we are

This verb is used for relations of identity and qualification (as with adjectives). Another verb, which can also be translated "to be," is used with the idea of presence, being in a place. Thus, ኢዩ would be used in sentences like "She is a woman" or "This book is new," but not in sentences like "The horse is in the meadow" or "The pen is on the table." A similar distinction between *ser* and *estar* is familiar to students of Spanish.

Sentences with ኢዩ:

እቲ ወረቐት ጸዓዳ ኢዩ። *The paper is white.*
እታ ኩዕሶ ከባብ ኢያ። *The ball is round.*
እቶም ሰብኡት ሓያላት ኢዮም። *The men are strong.*
እተን ቆልዑ ናእሽቱ ኢየን። *The children are small.*

The independent personal subject pronouns are as follows.

	Singular		Plural		Polite forms
3 m.	ንሱ	he	ንሳቶም	they	ንሶም
f.	ንሳ	she	ንሳተን	they	ንሰን
2 m.	ንስኻ	you	ንስኻትኩም	you	ንስኹም
f.	ንስኺ	you	ንስኻትክን	you	ንስኸን
1 c.	ኣነ	I	ንሕና	we	ንሳትና

The polite forms are used when talking about or addressing a person to whom one defers. One might compare the English forms "Your honor," "Her majesty," and the like. The polite forms may also be used as plurals. The rules for using one form rather than another are social conventions. As with Spanish "Usted" and "tú," or German "Sie" and "du," mistakes of usage can involve people's feelings. When in doubt, the polite or plural form is safe. The form ንሳትና exists but is little used.

As in Latin and Greek, verb forms in Tigrinya are grammatically complete without subject pronouns. The presence of the pronoun can indicate a certain emphasis.

ሓያል እዩ።   *He is strong.*
ንሱ ሓያል እዩ።   He *is strong.*

LESSON 7

Negative of the Verb "to be"

The present tense of the negative of "to be" is as follows:

	Singular		Plural	
3 m.	አይኮነን	he is not	አይኮኑን	they are not
f.	አይኮነተን	she is not	አይኮናን	they are not
2 m.	አይኮንካን	you are not	አይኮንኩምን	you are not
f.	አይኮንክን	you are not	አይኮንክንን	you are not
1 c.	አይኮንኩን	I am not	አይኮንናን	we are not

እዚ መጽሐፍ ዓብዪ አይኮነን። *This book is not large.*

እዚዶ ርሳስ እዩ፤ አይኮነን፣ ብርዒ እዩ። *Is this a pencil? No, it is a pen.*

The 1st person plural አይኮንናን *we are not*, is pronounced with stress on the final syllable. This is different from the 3rd person feminine plural, አይኮናን *they are not*, which has no such stress.

LESSON 8

"Give me" and "Show me"

Tigrinya imperatives are inflected for the person or persons addressed; that is, "Please give me" will use one verb form if the request is to a woman and another if it is to a man, and still others if it is to men or women, plural. Polite forms resemble the plurals.

The table below does not give a complete summary of imperative forms. Only one suffix, ኒ or "me," is shown. The forms for "give him," "give us," and so on, will use other suffixes.

give me	show me	Speaking to:
ሀበኒ	አርእየኒ	you (m.s.)
ሀብኒ	አርእዪኒ	you (f.s.)
ሀቡኒ	አርእዩኒ	you (m. pl. or polite)
ሀባኒ	አርእያኒ	you (f. pl. or polite)

ርሳስ ሀበኒ። *Give me the pencil* (to an equal or a younger person)

መጽሓፍ አርእዪኒ። *Show me the book* (to an older woman or group of women)

LESSON 9

Cardinal Numbers

Some of the written forms of the Tigrinya numbers are derived from letters of the Greek alphabet, e.g. B (beta, 2) Γ (gamma, 3). Today for most purposes "arabic" numerals, like those in the left-hand column, are used.

1	፩	ሓደ (m.) ሓንቲ (f.)
2	፪	ክልተ
3	፫	ሰለስተ
4	፬	ኣርባዕተ
5	፭	ሓሙሽተ
6	፮	ሽዱሽተ
7	፯	ሾብዓተ or ሸውዓተ
8	፰	ሾሞንተ
9	፱	ትሽዓተ
10	፲	ዓሰርተ
11	፲፩	ዓሰርተው ሓደ
12	፲፪	ዓሰርተው ክልተ
13	፲፫	ዓሰርተው ሰለስተ
14	፲፬	ዓሰርተው ኣርባዕተ
15	፲፭	ዓሰርተው ሓሙሽተ
16	፲፮	ዓሰርተው ሽዱሽተ
17	፲፯	ዓሰርተው ሸውዓተ
18	፲፰	ዓሰርተው ሾሞንተ
19	፲፱	ዓሰርተው ትሽዓተ
20	፳	ዕስራ
21	፳፩	ዕስራን ሓደን
22	፳፪	ዕስራን ክልተን
23	፳፫	ዕስራን ሰለስተን
30	፴	ሰላሳ

40	፵	አርብዓ
50	፶	ሓምሳ
60	፷	ስላ
70	፸	ሰብዓ
80	፹	ሰማንያ
90	፺	ተስዓ
100	፻	ሚእቲ
140	፻፵	ሚእትን አርብዓን
141	፻፵፩	ሚእትን አርብዓን ሓደን
358	፫፻፶፰	ሰለስተ ሚእትን ሓምሳን ሸሞንትን
1,000	፲፻	ሽሕ
1,273	፲፪፻፸፫	ሽሕን ክልተ ሚእትን ሰብዓን ሰለስተን

LESSON 10

The Calendar

The days of the week are:

Sunday	ሰንበት	from Hebrew שבת, *sabbath*
Monday	ሰኑይ	Semitic root for "two"
Tuesday	ሰሉስ	cf. ሰለስተ *three*
Wednesday	ረቡዕ	cf. ኣርባዕተ *four*
Thursday	ሓሙስ	cf. ሓሙሽተ *five*
Friday	ዓርቢ	cf. ዕራርቦ *sunset*
Saturday	ቀዳም	"first" or "prior" (to Sunday)

The months are:

ጥሪ	January	ሓምለ	July
ለካቲት	February	ነሓሰ	August
መጋቢት	March	መስከረም	September
ሚያዝያ	April	ጥቅምቲ	October
ግንቦት	May	ሕዳር	November
ሰነ	June	ታሕሳስ	December

The calendar in Eritrea is the Gregorian calendar, the usual calendar of the Western world, with the names of the months as above. These are the same names and order of months as in the traditional Ge'ez calendar, but in that calendar they do not correspond with Gregorian months. The Ge'ez calendar also has a thirteenth month of five days, called ጳጉሜን (Gk ἐπαγόμεναι, *intercalated*). In leap years, which occur one year before the Gregorian leap year, the thirteenth month is six days long, and the new year begins on 12 መስከረም.

If dates are given in the Ge'ez script, as on the title pages of books, it may be that they refer to the traditional calendar (ዓመተ ምሕረት or ዓ. ም.). To determine the Gregorian year, add seven or eight to the Ge'ez year. The traditional date written ፲፱፻፶፩ (1951), found on the cover of the ሰዋስው - ትግርኛ *Tigrinya Grammar* (Asmara: Franciscan Press), would thus be 1958 or 1959.

Eritrean holidays or anniversaries include:

10 ለካቲት፣ 1990	ሓርነት ከተማ ምጽዋዕ	
	Liberation of Massawa	
23 መጋቢት፣ 1977	ምሕራር ናቅፋ	
	Nakfa's Liberation	
24 ግንቦት፣ 1991	መዓልቲ ሓርነት ኤርትራ	
	Eritrean Liberation Day	
20 ሰነ	መዓልቲ ስውኣት ኤርትራ	
	Eritrean Martyrs' Day	
1 መስከረም፣ 1961	ባሕቲ መስከረም *First of September*	
	በዓል ሰውራ *Revolution Day* Beginning of the Eritrean Armed Struggle for Self-determination	
11 መስከረም	ርእሰ ዓመት ብኣቆጻጽራ ግእዝ *New Year in the Ge'ez calendar*	

LESSON 11

Telling Time

The traditional notation of time began at 6:00 p.m. Thus the first hour, ሰዓት ሓደ ናይ ምሸት, would be 7:00 p.m. This usage is not common today. Standard time or G.M.T. is normal. Especially in villages it may not be necessary to give an exact hour, and the divisions of the day are as follows:

ወጋሕታ	– from first light to sunrise
ንግሆ	– from sunrise to midmorning
ረፍዲ ቅድሚ ቀትሪ	– from mid-morning to noon
ፍርቂ መዓልቲ	– midday, noon
ቀትሪ	– from noon to early afternoon
ኣጋ ምሸት	– afternoon (2 to 5 p.m.)
ዕራርቦ	– from about 5 p.m. to sunset
ምሸት	– from sunset to dark (6 to 7 p.m.)
ለይቲ	– night
ፍርቂ ለይቲ	– midnight

Examples of questions and answers about the time of day are as follows:

ሰዓት ክንደይ ኮይኑ፧	What time is it?
or ሰዓት ክንደይ ኣሎ፧	
ሰዓት ክልተ ኮይኑ።	It is two o'clock.
ሰዓት ሰለስተን ፈረቓን ኮይኑ።	It is three-thirty.
ንሰዓት ሽውዓት ሓሙሽተ ደቒቅ ጉደል።	It is five minutes to seven.
ሰዓት ሽዱሽተን ርብዕን ኮይኑ።	It is six-fifteen.

Note that all times *after* the hour have ሰዓት; then the hour and minutes joined with the suffix pair −ን, −ን ; then ኮይኑ (*it has become*). Times *before* the hour have the preposition ን with ሰዓት, then the hour and minutes, then ጐደል (*it remains*). More literal translations for the last two sentences above would be:

ንሰዓት ሸውዓተ ሓሙሽተ ደቒቕ ጐደል፡፡	*To the seventh hour five minutes remain.*
ሰዓት ሽዱሽተን ርብዕን ኮይኑ፡፡	*The hour six and a quarter has arrived.*

LESSON 12

Present Tense of the Verb "to be present"

This verb is conjugated as follows:

Positive

	Singular			Plural	
3 m.	አሎ	he is	አለዉ	they are
f.	አላ	she is	አለዋ	they are
2 m.	አሎኻ	you are	አሎኹም	you are
f.	አሎኺ	you are	አሎኽን	you are
1	አሎኹ	I am	አሎና	we are

Negative

	Singular			Plural	
3 m.	የሎን	he is not	የለዉን	they are not
f.	የላን	she is not	የለዋን	they are not
2 m.	የሎኻን	you are not	የሎኹምን	you are not
f.	የሎኺን	you are not	የሎኽንን	you are not
1	የሎኹን	I am not	የሎናን	we are not

The use of this verb (አሎ) can be confused with that of እዩ *to be*, since both words are often translated the same in English. To decide whether a form of እዩ or አሎ should be used, add the word "present" to "is," and if it makes sense, አሎ will usually be correct. Permanently fixed objects (as a house or field) take a form of እዩ.

ንሱ ሓረስታይ እዩ። *He is a farmer*
እቲ ገዛ ቀረባ እዩ። *That house is near.*

For animate objects, the negative of አሎ, present tense, is supplied by የሎን. For inanimate objects the negative of the present tense is supplied by የልቦን, which is not conjugated.

ማይዶ አሎ፤ የልቦን።   *Is there water? —There is none.*

The use of አሎ as an auxiliary will be taken up in a later lesson.

LESSON 13

Common Prepositions

There are two kinds of prepositions, simple and compound. Simple prepositions of one radical, e.g. ብ *by*, ን *to*, are prefixed to nouns, pronouns, and adjectives; those of two or more radicals, e.g. ካብ *from*, ብዘይ *without*, are written as separate words. Compound prepositions consist of a simple preposition (usually ኣብ) plus another word, e.g. ኣብ ጥቓ *nearby*, ኣብ ቅድሚ *in front*, ኣብ ውሽጢ *inside*, ኣብ ልዕሊ *above*.

ብ *by* (mainly instrumental, but notice the examples)

    ብበቕሊ መጺኡ።   *He came by mule.*
    ብክልተ ሰዓት ክወድአ እየ።   *I will finish it in two hours.*
    ብከረን ኣቢሎም ናብ ናቕፋ ኣትዮም።   *They came to Nacfa by way of Keren.*

ን *for* (to the advantage or disadvantage of something or someone)

    እቲ መግቢ ንኽልቢ እዩ።   *The food is for the dog.*
    ጴጥሮስ ንሓው ሃሪሙዎ።   *Peter struck his brother.*

ናይ *of* (possessive)

    እቲ መጽሓፍ ናይ መምህር እዩ።   *It is the teacher's book.*

ምስ *with* (signifies association)

    ሃብተ ምስ ዮሃንስ መጺኡ።   *Habte came with Yohannes.*

ቅድሚ *ago, before* (temporal)

> ቅድሚ ክልተ ሰዓት ሓወይ መጺኡ። *My brother came two hours ago.*
>
> ጴጥሮስ ናብ መቓብር ቅድሚ ዮሃንስ አተወ። *Peter entered the tomb before John.*

ካብ *from*

> ካብ ከተማ መጺአ። *She came from the town.*

አብ *in, at*

> አብ ቤት ጽሕፈት አሎ። *He's at the office.*

ብዘይ *without*

> ብዘይ ከውን ተባኢሶም። *They fought for no reason.*
>
> ብዘይ ገንዘብ ዕዳጋ ከይዶም። *They went to the market without money.*

ናብ *to, toward*

> ናብ ሩባ ከይዱ። *He went to the river.*

LESSON 14

Compound Prepositions

The most common compound prepositions are:

ኣብ ቅድሚ *in front of*

    ኣብቲ ቅድሚ ገዛ ኦም ኣሎ። *In front of the house is a tree.*
    ኣብ ቅድሚ ባንክ ንራኸብ። *Let's meet in front of the bank.*

ኣብ ውሽጢ *inside*

    እቲ መንበር ኣብ ውሽጢ ገዛ ኣሎ። *The chair is inside the house.*

ኣብ ጥቓ *beside, near*

    እቲ ብርዒ ኣብ ጥቓ እቲ መጽሓፍ ኣሎ። *The pen is beside the book.*

ኣብ ልዕሊ *above, over, on, upon*

    በራድ ኣብ ልዕሊ እቶን ኣሎ። *The kettle is on the stove.*

ኣብ ትሕቲ *under, beneath, below*

    እቲ ቈልዓ ኣብ ትሕቲ ዓራት ኣሎ። *The child is under the bed.*

ኣብ ድሕሪ *behind, outside*

    እቲ ዒላ ኣብ ድሕሪ ገዛ ኣሎ። *The well is behind the house.*

LESSON 15

Pronominal Suffixes

In Tigrinya as in other Semitic languages the normal way of expressing someone's possession of something is to attach an abbreviation of the pronoun – "his," "her," etc. – to the thing possessed, e.g. ገዛ *house,* ገዛና *our house.* Thus a noun can have many suffixes, a different one for each person, gender, and number. By way of illustration:

	Singular		Plural	
3 m.	ገዛኡ	his house	ገዛኦም	their house
f.	ገዛኣ	her house	ገዛኤን	their house
2 m.	ገዛኻ	your house	ገዛኹም	your house
f.	ገዛኺ	your house	ገዛኽን	your house
1 c.	ገዛይ	my house	ገዛና	our house

The *plural* of "house" will have a paradigm of its own. The suffixes are the same, but often a vowel shift or other phonetic change is introduced when the suffixes are added.

	Singular		Plural	
3 m.	ገዛውቱ	his houses	ገዛውቶም	their houses
f.	ገዛውታ	her houses	ገዛውተን	their houses
2 m.	ገዛውትኻ	your houses	ገዛውትኹም	your houses
f.	ገዛውትኺ	your houses	ገዛውትክን	your houses
1 c.	ገዛውተይ	my houses	ገዛውትና	our houses

The literal translation "houses" may be misleading. The meaning of the expression "his houses" in Tigrinya is usually "his neighborhood." But for a landlord it could mean "his buildings."

Possessive Pronominal Endings

nouns ending in:	my	our	your m.s.	your f.s.	your m.pl.	your f.pl.	his	her	their m.pl.	their f.pl.
ደብዳቤ 5th	ይ	ɴ	ህ	ሺ	ኻ-ም	ኻን	ሁ	ኻ	ኻም	ኻን
ማዕድ 7th	ይ	ɴ	ህ	ሺ	ኻ-ም	ኻን	ሁ	ኻ	ኻም	ኻን
ሐመ 2nd	7th + ይ	ɴ	ህ	ሺ	ኻ-ም	ኻን	ሁ	ኻ	ኻም	ኻን
ዝ 4th	ይ	ɴ	ህ	ሺ	ኻ-ም	ኻን	ሁ	ኻ	ኻም	ኻን
አደ 1st	ይ	5th + ɴ	5th + ህ	5th + ሺ	5th + ኻ-ም	5th + ኻን	6th + ሁ	6th + ኻ	6th + ኻም	6th + ኻን
ዓጌ, ይ 3rd	1st + ይ	6th + ɴ	6th + ህ	6th + ሺ	6th + ኻ-ም	6th + ኻን	3rd + ሁ	3rd + ኻ	3rd + ኻም	3rd + ኻን
መፃሕይመ 6th	1st + ይ	ɴ	ህ	ሺ	ህም	ኽን	2nd	4th	7th + ም	1st + ን
	1st + ይ	ɴ	ህ	ሺ	ህም	ኽን	2nd	4th	7th + ም	1st + ን

35

LESSON 16

Possessive Pronouns

The possessive pronouns that are independent, or stand as separate words, are as follows:

	Singular		Plural		Polite Forms
3 m.	ናቱ	his	ናታቶም	their, theirs	ናቶም
f.	ናታ	her, hers	ናታተን	their, theirs	ናተን
2 m.	ናትካ	your, yours	ናታትኩም	your, yours	ናትኩም
f.	ናትኪ	your, yours	ናታትክን	your, yours	ናትክን
1 c.	ናተይ	my, mine	ናትና	our, ours	

The possessive pronouns can be used as adjectives. In this usage, they replace the pronominal suffixes, and there is a suggestion of stress or emphasis.

ናተይ መጽሓፍ ኣብዚ ኣሎ። *My book is here.*
መጽሓፊይ ኣብዚ ኣሎ። *My book is here.*

The pronoun can be made negative with the prefix ኣይ and suffix ን. But it would be more usual to make the verb negative.

ናትካ ዲዩ፧ ናተይ እዩ። *Is it yours? —It's mine.*
ናትካ ዲዩ፧ ናተይ ኣይኮነን። *Is it yours? —It isn't mine.*
or ኣይናተይን እዩ። *It is not mine.*

LESSON 17

The Verb

Semitic languages are generally understood to have as a distinguishing feature a predominance of triconsonantal roots which are articulated by the vowels and in other ways to form systems of words of related meaning. A common illustration is Arabic KTB from which are formed the words for "write," "book," "author," and so on. The Tigrinya vocabulary can be analyzed in this way. Thus the words ጸሓፈ *he wrote,* ጸሓፊ *writer,* መጽሓፍ *book,* seem to be formed from a common "root" ጸሓፊ with a "root meaning" of *write.* The Semitic languages, and certainly Tigrinya, invite such an analysis.

The verbs in Tigrinya could be taken as a thorough working out of a method in which a root, consisting usually of three radicals, is articulated in patterns which convey different meanings and applications of the verbal idea that belongs to the root. These patterns form subordinate systems with relatively consistent emphases of their own, such as "passive," "reflexive," "intensive," and so forth. The inflections of these systems give the tense and specify the person and number of subjects and objects.

The simplest form of a verb is generally the 3rd person masculine singular, simple perfect tense, e.g. ሰበረ *he broke.* This form is called the "root form" of the verb and is used as the name of the verb. In English, the infinitive is used to name verbs ("to be," "to go"); in Latin and Greek, the present tense, 1st person singular is used (e.g. Latin porto *I carry,* amo *I love*). These conventions are fixed by tradition.

The Basic Verb Families

Tigrinya verbs can be classified in "families" according to the nature of the radicals that they contain. Some of the families are subdivided into two "types" according to whether the second radical is geminated or "doubled." Such doubling affects the way that individual forms of a verb are derived from its basic consonantal root. The presence of certain letters or sounds, notably the laryngeals, also affects the production of forms. Verbs in a given class are changed in regular patterns to produce the tenses, aspects, persons, and so forth, that the verb forms can express. To conjugate a verb means to derive and list in order all the verb forms that belong to that verb. In English, the verbs themselves change very little. Conjugating is a matter of supplying auxiliary verbs and pronouns to a very few forms.

In Tigrinya there are many different forms. There are also auxiliaries. The five basic families and their subdivisions are as follows:

Family I
Verbs whose root form radicals are all written with 1st form vowels.

I, type A
The second radical is not doubled. (There is an exception in the imperfect when there is no final vowel. This means the word ends with a 6th form final, e.g. ይስብር *he breaks*.)
ቀተለ *kill*, ሰበረ *break*, ሐጸበ *wash*

I, type B
   The second radical is doubled.
   ፈጸመ *complete,* መረቀ *bless,* ረዳ *help*

Family II
   The third radical is *a laryngeal* or ይ or ው. (The laryngeals are
   አ, ዐ, ሀ, and ሐ.) This family has three subdivisions
   corresponding to these three possibilities. Each subdivision
   may be of type A or B, depending on gemination of the
   second radical.

II –1. Third radical is *a laryngeal.*
   II–1, type A
      በላ፤ *eat,* ሰርሐ *work,* በጽሐ *arrive*
   II–1, type B
      ወርሐ *spend the month,* ረስዐ *forget,* ተክአ *substitute,*
      ጸውዐ *call*

II –2. Third radical is ይ.
   II–2, type A
      ሰትይ *drink,* ዐበይ *grow,* ፈለይ *want,* ጠመይ *be hungry*
   II–2, type B
      ቀነይ *spend some time,* ጸለይ *pray,* ኮረይ *be angry*

II –3. Third radical is ው.
   II–3, type A
      ዐጸወ *close,* አተወ *enter,* ፈተወ *resemble*
   II–3, type B
      ፈነወ *loosen,* ሐለወ *guard,* ሐሰወ *lie*

Family III

The middle radical is *a laryngeal* or ፨ or ወ. This family also has three subdivisions corresponding to these three possibilities. A subdivision may be type A or B if the second radical can be geminated.

III –1. The middle radical is *a laryngeal* (አ, ዐ, ሀ, or ሐ).
Laryngeals cannot be doubled, so these are all of one type.
ጻሐፈ *write*, ጠዐመ *be sweet (taste)*, ለአከ *send*, ሰሐበ *pull*

III–2. The middle radical is ፨.
III–2, type A
ሆየ *go*, ሸጠ *sell*. The ፨ is a "weak" radical and is dropped in the perfect conjugation of this type of verb.
III–2, type B
ቀየረ *change*, ጸየፈ *stain*, ጠየፈ *inquire*

III–3. The middle radical is ወ.
III–3, type A
ዞረ *go around*, ጾረ *carry*, ሞተ *die*. In conjugating the perfect tense of this type of verb, a radical with a 1st form vowel is followed by ወ. The radical changes to 7th form, and ወ is dropped.
III–3, type B
ዘወረ *drive*, ለወጠ *change*, ከወለ *hide*

Verbs II–1, II–2, II–3, and III–2, III–3, are conjugated in the same patterns as family I, in the two types A and B. With few exceptions, the changes of spelling that occur happen for phonetic reasons when a laryngeal or ወ or ፨ is combined with the vowel of an adjacent radical. Verbs III–1 do not have types A and B and do not follow either pattern consistently.

Family IV

Verbs of four radicals, and not ending in ይ or ው . These verbs are classified as type C .

ገንደለ *unfold,* ደነገጸ *pity,* መስከረ *testify,* ቀልጠፈ *go quickly*

Family V

Verbs of four radicals ending in ይ or ው .These verbs are also of type C.

V–1. Four radicals ending in ይ .
ደርበይ *throw away*

V–2. Four radicals ending in ው .
ሰንደው *toss*

Family IV and V verbs are conjugated like verbs of type B in the other families, but the second radical stays in the 6th form and there is no doubling. In family V, the presence of ይ or ው causes phonetic changes.

Verb Families

Family			Type of Verb	Example	
I		A	3 radicals	ጸረገ	clear, clean
		B	3 radicals	ፈጸመ	complete
II	1	A	final *laryngeal*	በላዐ	eat
		B	final *laryngeal*	ረስዐ	forget
	2	A	final ይ	ሰተየ	drink
		B	final ይ	ቀነየ	spend some days
	3	A	final ወ	ዐጸወ	close
		B	final ወ	ፈነወ	loosen
III	1		middle *laryngeal*	ጸሐፈ	write
	2	A	middle ይ	ሐየ	go
		B	middle ይ	ቀየረ	change
	3	A	middle ወ	ሞተ	die
		B	middle ወ	ዘወረ	drive
IV			4 radicals	ገንጸለ	unfold
V	1		4 radicals, final ይ	ደርበየ	throw away
	2		4 radicals, final ወ	ሰንደወ	toss

Verb Types

Type A (middle radical not doubled) verbs are found in families I, II, III.

Type B (with doubling) are found in families I, II, III.

Type C is defined as including all verbs in families IV and V, and verbs with a primary internal change stem. "Primary Internal Change Stem" verbs are conjugated through internal changes instead of prefixes and suffixes. In these verbs, the first radical is 4th form and stays in this form throughout the conjugation, with an exception in the nounal infinitive. Verbs of this type are ባርኽ *bless* and ናፈቐ *long for*.

In Type A verbs, the second radical of the root form of the verb is doubled in the imperfect tense, when the final radical is without a vowel (that is, the final radical is in the 6th form and closes a syllable rather than beginning a new one).

Type B verbs have doubling throughout.

Type C verbs have no doubling. Also, Family III—1 has no doubling, because the laryngeals are not doubled.

Tigrinya spelling does not indicate where doubling, or "gemination," occurs. Here it is shown by two dots under the double letter.

LESSON 18

Simple Perfect of All Verb Families

The simple perfect expresses action accomplished in the past. It is used to narrate things that took place in the distant past:

ብመጀመርታ አምላከ ሰማይን ምድርን ፈጠረ።
In the beginning, God created heaven and earth.

It is seldom used in simple sentences in ordinary conversation. But it does have other important uses and they will be studied later.

The simple perfect of አረገ *clear* is as follows:

	Singular		Plural	
3 m.	አረገ	he cleared	አረጉ	they cleared
f.	አረገት	she cleared	አረጋ	they cleared
2 m.	አረግከ	you cleared	አረግኩም	you cleared
f.	አረግኪ	you cleared	አረግከን	you cleared
1 c.	አረግኩ	I cleared	አረግን	we cleared

The verb chart shows how to form the simple perfect tense of verbs representing each of the main types of verbs.

Simple Perfect Tense – Families I and II

Family Group – Type	I 1–A	I 1–B	II 1–A	II 1–B	II 2–A	II 2–B	II 3–A	II 3–B
እኔ	ዘረግኩ	ፈፀምኩት	ባለዕኩት	ረሰዕኩት	ሱቴኩት	ቀጌኩት	ገጸኩት	ፈናኩት
ንሕና	ዘረግና	ፈፀምና	ባለዕና	ረሰዕና	ሱቴና	ቀጌና	ዐጸና	ፈናና
ንስኻ	ዘረግካ	ፈፀምካ	ባለዕካ	ረሰዕካ	ሱቴካ	ቀጌካ	ዐጸካ	ፈናኻ
ንስኺ	ዘረግኪ	ፈፀምኪ	ባለዕኪ	ረሰዕኪ	ሱቴኪ	ቀጌኪ	ዐጸኪ	ፈናኺ
ንስኻትኩም	ዘረግኩም	ፈፀምኩም	ባለዕኩም	ረሰዕኩም	ሱቴኩም	ቀጌኩም	ዐጸኩም	ፈናኩም
ንስኻትኩን	ዘረግኩን	ፈፀምኩን	ባለዕኩን	ረሰዕኩን	ሱቴኩን	ቀጌኩን	ዐጸኩን	ፈናኩን
ንሱ	ዘረገ	ፈፀመ	ባለዐ	ረሰዐ	ሱቴዩ	ቀነየ	ዐጸወ	ፈነወ
ንሳ	ዘረገት	ፈፀመት	ባለዐት	ረሰዐት	ሱተዩት	ቀነየት	ዐጸወት	ፈነወት
ንስዩም	ዘረጉ	ፈፀሙ	ባለዑ	ረሰዑ	ሱተዩ	ቀነዩ	ዐጸዉ	ፈነዉ
ንስተን	ዘረጋ	ፈፀማ	ባለዓ	ረሰዓ	ሱተያ	ቀነያ	ዐጸዋ	ፈነዋ

45

Simple Perfect Tense – Families III, IV, and V

Family	III	III	III	III	III	IV	V	V
Group – Type	1–A	2–A	2–B	3–A	3–B		1	2
ኣነ	ጸሓፍኩ	ከድኩ	ቀየርኩ	ሞትኩ	ዘወርኩ	ገንጸልኩ	ደርቤኹ	ሰንዶኹ
ንሕና	ጸሓፍና	ከድና	ቀየርና	ሞትና	ዘወርና	ገንጸልና	ደርቤና	ሰንዶና
ንስኻ	ጸሓፍካ	ከድካ	ቀየርካ	ሞትካ	ዘወርካ	ገንጸልካ	ደርቤኻ	ሰንዶኻ
ንስኺ	ጸሓፍኪ	ከድኪ	ቀየርኪ	ሞትኪ	ዘወርኪ	ገንጸልኪ	ደርቤኺ	ሰንዶኺ
ንስኻትኩም	ጸሓፍኩም	ከድኩም	ቀየርኩም	ሞትኩም	ዘወርኩም	ገንጸልኩም	ደርቤኹም	ሰንዶኹም
ንስኻትክን	ጸሓፍክን	ከድክን	ቀየርክን	ሞትክን	ዘወርክን	ገንጸልክን	ደርቤኽን	ሰንዶኽን
ንሱ	ጸሓፈ	ከደ	ቀየረ	ሞተ	ዘወረ	ገንጸለ	ደርበየ	ሰንደወ
ንሳ	ጸሓፈት	ከደት	ቀየረት	ሞተት	ዘወረት	ገንጸለት	ደርበየት	ሰንደወት
ንሳቶም	ጸሓፉ	ከዱ	ቀየሩ	ሞቱ	ዘወሩ	ገንጸሉ	ደርበዩ	ሰንደዉ
ንሳተን	ጸሓፋ	ከዳ	ቀየራ	ሞታ	ዘወራ	ገንጸላ	ደርበያ	ሰንደዋ

LESSON 19

Simple Imperfect of All Verb Families

The Tigrinya imperfect is used for actions that are incomplete or customary. By itself, the imperfect expresses what is customary or usual. For example,

ሰብ ይምነ፡ እዝጊ ይፍጽም።
Man proposes, God disposes.

አብ ተዋስኦ ይሰርሕ።
He works in the theater.

The simple imperfect together with the corresponding form of the helping verb ኣሎ expresses actions taking place in the present.

ንሱ ሕጂ ይሰርሕ ኣሎ።
He is working now.

አብ ውሻጠ ይድቅስ ኣሎ።
He's sleeping in the back.

አብ ጽርግያ ባንዴራ የንበልብሉ ኣለው።
They're stringing banners over the road.

The verb chart shows how to form the simple imperfect tense of verbs representing each of the main types of verbs.

Imperfect Tense – Families I and II

Family Group – Type	I 1–A	I 1–B	II 1–A	II 1–B	II 2–A	II 2–B	II 3–A	II 3–B
እነ	እጸርግ	እፈጽም	እበልዕ	እርስዕ	እሰቲ	እቅጺ	እግዱ	እፉት
ንሕና	ንጸርግ	ንፈጽም	ንበልዕ	ንርስዕ	ንሰቲ	ንቅጺ	ንግዱ	ንፉት
ንስኻ	ትጸርግ	ትፈጽም	ትበልዕ	ትርስዕ	ትሰቲ	ትቅጺ	ትግዱ	ትፉት
ንስኺ	ትጸርጊ	ትፈጽሚ	ትበልዒ	ትርስዒ	ትሰቲዪ	ትቅጽዪ	ትግዲዪ	ትፉንዪ
ንስኻትኩም	ትጸርጉ	ትፈጽሙ	ትበልዑ	ትርስዑ	ትሰቱ	ትቅጹ	ትግዱው	ትፉንው
ንስኻትክን	ትጸርጋ	ትፈጽማ	ትበልዓ	ትርስዓ	ትሰታያ	ትቅጻያ	ትግዳዋ	ትፉንዋ
ንሱ	ይጸርግ	ይፈጽም	ይበልዕ	ይርስዕ	ይሰቲ	ይቅጺ	ይግዱ	ይፉት
ንሳ	ትጸርግ	ትፈጽም	ትበልዕ	ትርስዕ	ትሰቲ	ትቅጺ	ትግዱ	ትፉት
ንሳቶም	ይጸርጉ	ይፈጽሙ	ይበልዑ	ይርስዑ	ይሰቱ	ይቅጹ	ይግዱው	ይፉንው
ንሳተን	ይጸርጋ	ይፈጽማ	ይበልዓ	ይርስዓ	ይሰታያ	ይቅጻያ	ይግዳዋ	ይፉንዋ

Imperfect Tense — Families III, IV, and V

Family Group – Type	III 1–A	III 2–A	III 2–B	III 3–A	III 3–B	IV	V 1	V 2
እነ	እጸሕፍ	እከይድ	እቅይር	እመውት	እዘውር	እንገጽል	እድርስ	እስንዱ
ንሕና	ንጸሕፍ	ንከይድ	ንቅይር	ንመውት	ንዘውር	ንንገጽል	ንድርስ	ንስንዱ
ንስኻ	ትጸሕፍ	ትከይድ	ትቅይር	ትመውት	ትዘውር	ትንገጽል	ትድርስ	ትስንዱ
ንስኺ	ትጸሕፊ	ትከዪ	ትቅይሪ	ትሞቲ	ትዘሪ	ትንገጽሲ	ትድርብዪ	ትስንዱዊ
ንስኻትኩም	ትጸሕፉ	ትከዱ	ትቅይሩ	ትሞቱ	ትዘሩ	ትንገጽሱ	ትድርብዩ	ትስንዱው
ንስኻትክን	ትጸሕፋ	ትከዳ	ትቅይራ	ትሞታ	ትዘራ	ትንገጽና	ትድርብያ	ትስንዱቅ
ንሱ	ይጸሕፍ	ይከይድ	ይቅይር	ይመውት	ይዘውር	ይንገጽል	ይድርስ	ይስንዱ
ንሳ	ትጸሕፍ	ትከይድ	ትቅይር	ትመውት	ትዘውር	ትንገጽል	ትድርስ	ትስንዱ
ንሳቶም	ይጸሕፉ	ይከዱ	ይቅይሩ	ይሞቱ	ይዘሩ	ይንገጽሱ	ይድርብዩ	ይስንዱው
ንሳተን	ይጸሕፋ	ይከዳ	ይቅይራ	ይሞታ	ይዘራ	ይንገጽና	ይድርብያ	ይስንዱቅ

49

LESSON 20

Gerundive

The gerundive is the tense customarily used to express completed action. It can be used in the main clause of a sentence as the equivalent of the English present perfect:

ናብ መዓርፎ ነፈርቲ ከይዱ።   *He has gone to the airport.*

Narratives of the remote past use the simple perfect tense in Tigrinya. Otherwise, the gerundive is the equivalent of the English past tense.

ሓወይ ናብ ባጽዕ ከይዱ።   *My brother went to Massawa.*
ናይ ሕክምና ሓገዝ ረኺቦም።   *They received medical asssistance.*

Verbs which have a final ወ, or a middle ወ not doubled, change the ወ to ይ in the conjugation of this tense.

The gerundive of ነገረ *say* or *tell* is as follows:

	Singular		Plural	
3 m.	ነጊሩ	he said	ነጊሮም	they said
f.	ነጊራ	she said	ነጊረን	they said
2 m.	ነጊርካ	you said	ነጊርኩም	you said
f.	ነጊርኪ	you said	ነጊርክን	you said
1 c.	ነጊረ	I said	ነጊርና	we said

LESSON 21

Gerundive in Subordinate Clauses

Many actions that would be expressed in English by using a series of coordinate clauses are expressed in Tigrinya with the gerundive as a kind of subordinate clause, followed by the main verb.

ናብ በረኻ ከይዶም ዕንጨይቲ ይኣርዩ አለዉ። *They have gone into the wilderness and are picking up wood* (lit. *Having gone into the wilderness they are picking up wood*)

በሊዖምን ሰትዮምን ይኸዱ አለዉ። *They have eaten and drunk and are going* (lit. *Having eaten and drunk they are going*)

መጽሓፍካ ከፊትካ ኮፍ በል። *Open your book and sit down* (lit. *Having opened your book sit down*)

The gerundive has other uses that will be studied later.

LESSON 22

Imperative–Jussive

The imperative–jussive stem of the Tigrinya verb is fully conjugated. In English, the imperative is used only for the second person. For example, ናብ ሩባ ኪድኪ ማይ ኣምጽኢ። *Go to the river and bring water* is addressed to "you," second person feminine, and can be translated directly into English. But an imperative in the first person ("I," "we") or third person ("he," "she," "it," "they") may have to be translated with such a phrase as "let them" or "let us." Here, "let" means "may it happen," not "allow them" or "permit us." Other names for the "imperative" and "jussive" moods are "hortatory," and "cohortative." There is a "cohortative" in Hebrew and a "hortatory subjunctive" in Latin.

ናብ ደገ ንኺድ። *Let's go outside.*
ሕጉስ እንተሎ ይዘምር። *If anyone is happy, let him sing.*
ጸጋ ምስ ኩላትኩም ይኹን። *Grace be with you all.*
ነቲ ፈረስ ኣብቲ ዓንዲ እሰሮ። *Tie the horse to the pillar.*

The imperative–jussive of ረስዐ is as follows:

	Singular		Plural	
3 m.	ይረስዕ	*let him forget*	ይረስዑ	*let him forget*
f.	ትረስዕ	*let her forget*	ይረስዓ	*let them forget*
2 m.	ረስዕ	*forget!*	ረስዑ	*forget!*
f.	ረስዒ	*forget!*	ረስዓ	*forget!*
1 c.	እረስዕ	*let me forget*	ንረስዕ	*let us forget*

LESSON 23

Future Tense

The future tense is formed from the simple imperfect by adding the prefix ክ and using the appropriate form of እዩ *to be* as an auxiliary verb.

ሓወይ ጽባሕ ኪመጽእ እዩ። *My brother will come tomorrow.*
ማርያም ማይ ክትቀድሕ እያ። *Mariam will draw water.*

The verb ገብረ *make* or *do* is conjugated in the future as follows:

Singular

3 m.	ኪገብር	እዩ	he will do
f.	ክትገብር	እያ	she will do
2 m.	ክትገብር	ኢኻ	you will do
f.	ክትገብሪ	ኢኺ	you will do
1 c.	ክገብር	እየ	I will do

Plural

3 m.	ኪገብሩ	እዮም	they will do
f.	ኪገብራ	እየን	they will do
2 m.	ክትገብሩ	ኢኹም	you will do
f.	ክትገብራ	ኢኽን	you will do
1 c.	ክንገብር	ኢና	we will do

The prefix ክ becomes ኪ when the verb form to which it is prefixed begins with ይ. This occurs in three of the four third person forms above.

LESSON 24

Negative of All Tenses

The verb is made negative in Tigrinya by the addition of a prefix ኢይ and a suffix ን, or in other words, by adding ኢይ...ን to the inflection of the word. Many verbs have object pronouns suffixed to them, but the suffix ን comes last, e.g. ኢይመስለካን *It doesn't seem so to you.*

When the verb already begins with ይ, a second ይ is not added. Thus the negative of ይገብር *he is doing* is ኢይገብርን *he is not doing*, rather than *ኢይይገብርን.

When the verb form begins with ኣ, the resulting *ኣኢይ becomes ኣየ. Thus the negative of ኣቅትል *I cause to kill* is ኣየቅትልን *I am not causing to kill.*

For a negative command, the prefix is ኢይት and the letter ን is not added at the end. Thus the negative of ንገር *say* is ኢይትንገር *don't say.*

For the jussive, ኢይ is prefixed to the jussive form.

Note: an asterisk * marks forms given as examples only, and not found in the language.

LESSON 25

Infinitives, Adverbial and Nounal

The Tigrinya *adverbial* infinitive is formed by adding the prefix ከ to the simple imperfect. This is the same form as the future without the auxiliary verb. The adverbial infinitive can be translated with an English infinitive, as in the examples.

    ትግርኛ ክምሃር እደሊ ኣሎኹ።   *I want to learn Tigrinya.*
    ሓንቲ ሰበይቲ ማይ ክትቀድሕ መጸአ።   *A woman came to draw water.*

The Tigrinya *nounal* infinitive is formed by prefixing ም to the verb, after changing all its radicals to the 6th form, but the next to the last radical to the 4th. Thus for the verb ቀተለ the nounal infinitive is ምቅታል. For ደርበየ the nounal infinitive is ምድርባይ.

This form is used like English infinitives and gerunds.

    ምፍላስ መሬት የልምዕ።   *Sowing makes the ground lush.*
    ምጉሓፍ ክልኩል እዩ።   *Throwing trash is forbidden.*
    ምሕያኽ ብዕሪር ኣይፍቀድን እዩ።   *To chew gum is not allowed.*

LESSON 26

The Verb "to have"

"To have something" is expressed by an appropriate form of አሎ with an object suffix attached to it. That is, "I have the book" would be መጽሐፍ አሎኒ (lit) *The book is to me*. Object suffixes as such will be studied in a later lesson. Even so, one can see in the examples below that the pronoun object suffixes work like other inflections for gender and person: *he she you I* and so on.

In this use of አሎ, the verb is inflected to agree with its subject, which is the thing possessed. This usage is like the Latin dative of possession, e.g. *liber mihi est*, translated *I have the book*, but more literally, *The-book to-me is*. The verb agrees with "book," not "I."

አብዑር አለዉኒ።	I have oxen.
አሕ አለዋኒ።	I have cows.
አጣል አለዋና።	We have goats.
አኽላባት አለዉኺን።	You (f.p.) have dogs.
መጽሐፍ አሎኒ።	I have a book.
ላም አላትኒ።	I have a cow.
አብዑር አለዉኒ።	I have oxen.
አሕ አለዋኒ።	I have cows.
መጽሐፍ አሎካ።	You (m.s.) have a book.
መጽሐፍ አሎኪ።	You (f.s.) have a book.
መጽሐፍ አሎኩም።	You (m.pl.) have a book.
መጽሐፍ አሎክን።	You (f.pl.) have a book.
መጽሐፍ አሎና።	We have a book.
ላም አላትና።	We have a cow.
አብዑር አለዉና።	We have oxen.
አሕ አለዋና።	We have cows.

ላም አላትካ።	You (m.s.) have a cow.
ላም አላትኪ።	You (f.s.) have a cow.
ላም አላትኩም።	You (m.pl.) have a cow.
ላም አላትከን።	You (f.pl.) have a cow.
አብዑር አለዉኻ።	You (m.s.) have oxen.
አብዑር አለዉኺ።	You (f.s.) have oxen.
አብዑር አለዉኹም።	You (m.pl.) have oxen.
አብዑር አለዉኸን።	You (f.pl.) have oxen.
አሓ አለዋኻ።	You (m.s.) have cows.
አሓ አለዋኺ።	You (f.s.) have cows.
አሓ አለዋኹም።	You (m.pl.) have cows.
አሓ አለዋኸን።	You (f.pl.) have cows.
መጽሓፍ አለዎ።	He has a book.
ላም አላቶ።	He has a cow.
አብዑር አለዉዋ።	He has oxen.
አሓ አለዋእ።	He has cows.
መጽሓፍ አለዋ።	She has a book.
ላም አላታ።	She has a cow.
አብዑር አለዉዋ።	She has oxen.
አሓ አለዋእ።	She has cows.
መጽሓፍ አለዎም።	They (m.) have a book.
ላም አላቶም።	They (m.) have a cow.
አብዑር አለዉዎም።	They (m.) have oxen.
አሓ አለዋእም።	They (m.) have cows.
መጽሓፍ አለወን።	They (f.) have a book.
ላም አላተን።	They (f.) have a cow.
አብዑር አለዉወን።	They (f.) have oxen.
አሓ አለዋኤን።	They (f.) have cows.

LESSON 27

Negative of the Verb "to have"

The negative of the verb "to have" is inflected for the person or persons that has or does not have, by changing the pronominal suffixes. But it is not inflected for the grammatical subject, the things possessed. The same verb would be used in "I don't have cows" and "I don't have oxen." But the verb would change in its suffix if "I" were to become "we."

The conjugation of "not to have" is as follows:

	Singular		Plural	
3 m.	የብሉ፞	he doesn't have	የብሉ፞ም፞	they don't have
f.	የብላ፞	she doesn't have	የብለን፞	they don't have
2 m.	የብልክ፞	you don't have	የብሉ፞ም፞	you don't have
f.	የብልሽ፞	you don't have	የብልኝ፞	you don't have
1 c.	የብለይ፞	I don't have	የብላን፞	we don't have

LESSON 28

Object Suffixes in Simple Perfect

The Tigrinya object suffixes are personal pronouns suffixed to verbs. The use of object pronouns in Tigrinya is not exactly like that of English, although translation is usually not difficult. As in English, a verb can have both a direct and an indirect object. Thus, "Show me the pen" has an indirect object "me" and a direct object "pen." In Tigrinya, the pronoun "me" becomes part of the verb and is not written separately: ኣርኣየኒ *Show me*.

The object suffixes in the following charts, used with a verb like ሓገዘ *help*, would be equivalent to an English direct object: ሓገዘኒ *Help me*. The same suffix occurs in ኣርኣየኒ *Show me*. In English grammar, this "me" could be called an indirect object, as in "Show me the book," although the Tigrinya construction is the same. In other words, the object suffixes in Tigrinya are not always the same as "direct objects" in English. Other kinds of objects in Tigrinya, which correspond more closely to the English indirect object, will be studied later.

	Singular			Plural	
3 m.	7th form	*him*	7th + ም		*them*
f.	4th form	*her*	1st + ን		*them*
2 m.	ካ	*you*	ክ-ም		*you*
f.	ኪ	*you*	ክን		*you*
1 c.	ኒ	*me*	ና		*us*

The suffixes are added to the verbs with some adjustments:

Verbs feminine in ን change to ና before adding the suffix.
All 3rd forms change to 6th before adding the suffix.
In the gerundive 3 fem. sg., ት is added before the suffix.
Before the 1st or 2d person suffix, a final radical 6th form changes to a 1st form.

Addition of the suffixes for the 3rd person is more involved. The following general rules should be interpreted with the help of the charts, and vice-versa.

> 1st and 6th forms of the stem change to the required vowel. Exception: some gerundives add ኡ .
>
> 2d of stem plus 6th – add ወ with the proper vowel.
>
> 3rd of stem plus 6th – add ዩ with the proper vowl.
>
> 4th of stem – add አ , except in the gerundive 3 fem. sg., which adds ት with the proper vowel.
>
> Personal 4th endings ከ and ና – add ዩ with proper vowel.
>
> Personal masc. ም – add ወ with proper vowel.
>
> Personal fem. ን – add አ with proper vowel.

Simple Perfect Tense, with Singular Object Suffixes

singular suffixes:	me	you, m.sg.	you, f.sg.	him	her
I –1 sing.		ገድፉትኻ	ገድፉትኺ	ገድፉትዎ	ገድፉትዋ
we –1 pl.		ገድፍናኻ	ገድፍናኺ	ዳናዮ	ዳናያ
you –2 m.sg.	ገድፍካኒ			ገድፍካዮ	ገድፍካያ
you –2 f.sg.	ገድፍኪኒ			ገድፍክዮ	ገድፍክያ
you –2 m.pl.	ገድፍኩምኒ			ገድፍኩምዎ	ገድፍኩምዋ
you –2 f.pl.	ገድፍክንኒ			ገድፍክንኦ	ገድፍክንኣ
he –3 m.sg.	ገደፈኒ	ገደፈኻ	ገደፈኺ	ገደፎ	ገደፋ
she –3 f.sg.	ገደፈትኒ	ገደፈትካ	ገደፈትኪ	ገደፈቶ	ገደፈታ
they –3 m.pl.	ገደፉኒ	ገደፉኻ	ገደፉኺ	ገደፉዎ	ገደፉዋ
they –3 f.pl.	ገደፋኒ	ገደፋኻ	ገደፋኺ	ገደፋኦ	ገደፋኣ

Simple Perfect Tense, with Plural Object Suffixes

plural suffixes:	us	you, m.pl.	you, f.pl.	them, m.pl.	them, f.pl.
I −1 sing.		ገድፌአችኹም	ገድፌአችኽን	ገድፌአቸዋም	ገድፌአቸዋን
we −1 pl.		ገድፈናችኹም	ገድፈናችኽን	ገድፈናቸም	ገድፈናቸን
you −2 m.sg.	ገድፈኸን			ገድፈኸያም	ገድፈኸያን
you −2 f.sg.	ገድፈሽን			ገድፈሽያም	ገድፈሽያን
you −2 m.pl.	ገድፋችኹወን			ገድፋችኹዋም	ገድፋችኹዋን
you −2 f.pl.	ገድፋችኽን			ገድፋችኽአም	ገድፋችኽአን
he −3 m.sg.	ገድፈን	ገድፈኻም	ገድፈከን	ገድፈያም	ገድፈያን
she −3 f.sg.	ገድፈችን	ገድፈቻችኹም	ገድፈቻችኽን	ገድፈቻም	ገድፈቻን
they −3 m.pl.	ገድፉን	ገድፉኻም	ገድፉከን	ገድፉያም	ገድፉዋን
they −3 f.pl.	ገድፉን	ገድፉኻም	ገድፉከን	ገድፉአም	ገድፉአን

Imperfect Tense, with Singular Object Suffixes

subject	obj.	3m him, them	3f her, them	2m you, m.	2f you, f.	1c me, us
he	sg.	ይግድፍ	ይግድፉ	ይግድፈህ	ይግድፈኪ	ይግድፈኒ
	pl.	ይግድፎም	ይግድፈን	ይግድፈህም	ይግድፈክን	ይግድፈና
she	sg.	ትግድፍ	ትግድፉ	ትግድፈህ	ትግድፈኪ	ትግድፈኒ
	pl.	ትግድፎም	ትግድፈን	ትግድፈህም	ትግድፈክን	ትግድፈና
you, m. sg.	sg.	ትግድፍ	ትግድፉ			ትግድፈኒ
	pl.	ትግድፎም	ትግድፈን			ትግድፈና
you, f. sg.	sg.	ትግድፍዮ	ትግድፍያ			ትግድፍኒ
	pl.	ትግድፍዮም	ትግድፍየን			ትግድፍያና
I	sg.	እግድፍ	እግድፉ	እግድፈህ	እግድፈኪ	
	pl.	እግድፎም	እግድፈን	እግድፈህም	እግድፈክን	

63

Imperfect Tense, with Plural Object Suffixes

subject	obj.	3m him, them	3f her, them	2m you, m.	2f you, f.	1c me, us
they, m.	sg.	ይነድፉዋ	ይነድፉዋ	ይነድፉኻ	ይነድፉኺ	ይነድፉኒ
	pl.	ይነድፉዎም	ይነድፉዎን	ይነድፉኻም	ይነድፉኺን	ይነድፉና
they, f.	sg.	ይነድፋኣ	ይነድፋኣ	ይነድፋኻ	ይነድፋኺ	ይነድፋኒ
	pl.	ይነድፋኦም	ይነድፋኤን	ይነድፋኻም	ይነድፋኺን	ይነድፋና
you, m. pl.	sg.	ትነድፉዋ	ትነድፉዋ			ትነድፉኒ
	pl.	ትነድፉዎም	ትነድፉዎን			ትነድፉና
you, f. pl.	sg.	ትነድፋኣ	ትነድፋኣ			ትነድፋኒ
	pl.	ትነድፋኦም	ትነድፋኤን			ትነድፋና
we	sg.	ንነድፎ	ንነድፋ	ንነድፈካ	ንነድፈኪ	
	pl.	ንነድፎም	ንነድፈን	ንነድፈካም	ንነድፈክን	

LESSON 29

More Prepositions and Pronoun Objects

Some more prepositions (continuing Lesson 14):

ከም *like*

ኢዮብ ከም አቡኡ ሓያል እዩ። *Job is strong like his father.*

ኣብ ክንዲ *instead of, in exchange for*

ኣብ ክንዲ ፈረሰይ እዚ ብዕራይ ሃበኒ። *Give me this ox in exchange for my horse.*

ምእንቲ *for the sake of, for*

ምእንቲ አደይ መጺኤ። *I have come for my mother's sake.*

ስለ *for the sake of*

ክርስቶስ ስለና ሞተ። *Christ died for our sakes.*

ብዛዕባ *concerning, about*

ብዛዕባ ዛንታ ኤርትራ ተዛራሪብና። *We spoke about the history of Eritrea.*

ስጋብ *as far as, until* (**ክሳዕ** also occurs)

ስጋብ ጽባሕ ክንጸንሕ ኢና። *We will stay until tomorrow.*

ሳላ *thanks to*

ሳላኹም ስራሕ ረኺበ። *Thanks to you, I found work.*

ብሰሪ *by fault of* or **ብሰንኪ**

ብሰሪ ሓጢኣት ጠፊእና። *Because of sin, we are lost.*
ብሰንኪ ንቑጽ ይነድድ ርሑስ። *Because [some of it is] dry, the wet will burn.*

65

Prepositions are often used with personal pronoun suffixes. Thus "to, or toward, me" is ናብ + ኣነ , that is, ናባይ . Below are declensions of preposition and suffix for ን *to* or *for;* ብዛዕባ *about;* ምስ *with;* and ባዕሉ *alone, by oneself.*

	Singular		Plural	
3 m.	ንዕኡ	to him	ንዕኦም	to them
f.	ንዕኣ	to her	ንዕኤን	to them
2 m.	ንኣኻ	to you	ንኣኹም	to you
f.	ንኣኺ	to you	ንኣኽን	to you
1 c.	ንኣይ	to me	ንኣና	to us

	Singular		Plural	
3 m.	ብዛዕብኡ	about him	ብዛዕብኦም	about them
f.	ብዛዕብኣ	about her	ብዛዕብኤን	about them
2 m.	ብዛዕባኻ	about you	ብዛዕባኹም	about you
f.	ብዛዕባኺ	about you	ብዛዕባኽን	about you
1 c.	ብዛዕባይ	about me	ብዛዕባና	about us

	Singular		Plural	
3 m.	ምስኡ	with him	ምስኦም	with them
f.	ምስኣ	with her	ምስኤን	with them
2 m.	ምሳኻ	with you	ምሳኹም	with you
f.	ምሳኺ	with you	ምሳኽን	with you
1 c.	ምሳይ	with me	ምሳና	with us

	Singular		Plural	
3 m.	ባዕሉ	by himself	ባዕሎም	by themselves
f.	ባዕላ	by herself	ባዕለን	by themselves
2 m.	ባዕልኻ	by yourself	ባዕልኹም	by yourselves
f.	ባዕልኺ	by yourself	ባዕልኽን	by yourselves
1 c.	ባዕለይ	by myself	ባዕልና	by ourselves

LESSON 30

Adverbs

Some commonly used adverbs:

ሎም ቅነ *very recently, soon*
   ሎም ቅነ ማይ ሀሪሙ። *It rained very recently.*

ሎም ዘበን *this year*
   ሎም ዘበን ሓዉ ተመርዕዩ። *His brother married this year.*

መኣስ *when* (or **መኣዝ**)
   መኣዝ መጺእካ፧ *When did you come?*

ሎሚ *today*
   ሎሚ ክዳውንቲ ሓጺበ። *I washed clothes today.*

ጽባሕ *tomorrow*
   ጽባሕ ዕዳጋ ክወርድ እየ። *Tomorrow I will go to market.*

ድሕሪ ጽባሕ *day after tomorrow*

ትማሊ *yesterday*

ቅድሚ ትማሊ *day before yesterday* (also **ብቕድሚ ትማሊ**)

ትማሊ ሓሙስ *last Thursday*

ዓሚ *last year*

ሕጂ *now*
   እቲ ገንዘብ ሕጂ ክህበካ እየ። *I'll give you that money now.*

ገና *not yet* (or **ጌና**)

    እታ አውቶቡስ ገና አይመጸትን። *Still the bus hasn't arrived.*

ሽዑ *then, next*

    ሽዑ ናብ በረኻ ወጸኣ። *Next he went into the field.*

ቅድም *before, earlier*

    ነቲ ስራሕ ቅድም ፈጺሙ። *He finished the work before.*

ድሓር *later, then*

    ድሓር ክንራኸብ ኢና። *We'll get together later.*

ኩሉ ሳዕ *always* (the usual word; also **ኩሉ ሻዕ**)

    ኩሉ ሳዕ የንብብ። *Always he is reading.*

ወትሩ *always* (less commonly; also **ወርትግ**)

    ወትሩ ዕዉት። *He is always victorious.*

ከቶ *never, absolutely not*

    ከቶ አይንምብርከኽን። *We never kneel down.*

አበይ *where?*

    አበይ አሎኻ፧ *Where are you?*

ካበይ *from where?*

    ካበይ መጺእካ፧ *From where did you come?*

አብዚ *here*

    ብዙሓት መካይን አብዚ አለዋ። *There are a lot of cars here.*

አብኡ *there*

    ጥንታዊ ህንጻ አብኡ አሎ። *An ancient building is there.*

አብ ው-ሽጢ *inside*

አብ ው-ሽጢ እቲ አጉዶ ቄልዓ አሎ። *Inside that hut is a child.*

አብ ላዕሊ *above* (the spelling differs when used alone and when followed by a noun)

አብ ልዕሊ ነፋሲት ቢዘን ትረክብ። *Above Nefasit you find Bizen.*
እቲ ማይ ካብ ላዕሊ ወሪዱ። *The water came from above.*

አብ ታሕቲ *below*

ክፉአ ዝገብር አብ ታሕቲ ይነብር። *Those who do evil live in an inferior way.*

ንየው *far*

እተን አሓ ንየው በለን። *Drive the cattle away.*

ነጀው *near*

ነቲ መሓስእ ነጀው አብሎ። *Bring the kid to me.*

ንየው ... ነጀው *here and there*

እቲ ጽሉል ንየው ነጀው ይብል አሎ። *The insane person is going here and there.*

ካብ ንየው *beyond* (also **ካብ ኔው**)

ክነጀው *this side*

ጽቡቕ *well*

ጽቡቕ ገይሩ። *He did well.*

ክፉእ *poorly, badly*

ክፉእ ሰሪሑ። *He worked badly.*

ብፍጹም *truly, completely, surely*

    ብፍጽም አይተዛረበን፡፡   *He said nothing at all.*

ብሐቂ *in truth*

    ብሐቂ ንገረኒ፡፡   *Tell me truly.*

ጥራይ *only*

    ሓንቲ ደርሆ ጥራይ ረኺቦም፡፡   *They found only one hen.*

በይኑ *alone*

    በይኑ መጺኡ፡፡   *He came alone.*

ምናዳ *particularly, especially*

    እዞም ተምሃሮ ንፉዓት እዮም፣ ምናዳ ኤጥሮስ፡፡   *Those students are clever, especially Peter.*

ኣስታት *about, approximately*

    ዕድሚኡ ኣስታት ሓምሳ ዓመት ይኸውን፡፡   *His age is about fifty.*

ኣቢሉ *about, approximately* (the more usual expression)

    ዕድሚኡ ሓምሳ ዓመት ኣቢሉ ይኸውን፡፡   *His age is about fifty.*

ከመይ *how?*

    ከመይ ውዒልኩም፧   *How did you spend the day?* (i.e. Good afternoon)

Often adverbs of manner are constructed by using a noun with the prefix **ብ** .

ብሕያውነት ተቐቢሉና።   *He received us warmly.*

There are verbs which may be used in the gerundive as finite verbs, but which would naturally be translated with adverbs.

አጸቢቆም ይጽሕፉ።   *They are writing neatly.*
አቐዲመ ከውርየልኩም።   *First I'll tell you the news.*
ቀልጢፎም ገይሮሞ።   *They did it quickly.*

Some expressions of affirmation and negation are as follows.

እወ   *yes*
ሕራይ   *all right*
እሺ   *yes, all right*
ድሓን   *okay, fine*
አቤት   *at your service*
እምቢ   *no!* (strong refusal)
እንድዒ   *I don't know* (somewhat impolite)
ምናልባት   *maybe*
ይኸውን   *it could be*
አይከውንን እዩ።   *It's not possible.*

Common Adverbs

For the convenience of the reader, the adverbs in Lesson 30 are presented together below.

ሎም ቅነ	very recently, soon	አብዚ	here
ሎም ዘበን	this year	አብኡ	there
መኣስ	when	አብ ውሽጢ	inside
ጽባሕ	tomorrow	አብ ላዕሊ	above
ድሕሪ ጽባሕ	day after tomorrow	አብ ታሕቲ	below
ትማሊ	yesterday	ንየው	far
ቅድሚ ትማሊ	day before yesterday	ነጀው	near
ትማሊ ሓሙስ	last Thursday	ንየው...ነጀው	here and there
ዓሚ	last year	ካብ ንየው	beyond
ሕጂ	now	ክነጀው	this side
ገና	not yet	ጽቡቕ	well
ሽዑ	then, next	ክፉእ	poorly, badly
ቅድም	before, earlier	ብፍጹም	truly, completely, surely
ድሓር	later, then	ብሓቂ	in truth
ኩሉ ሳዕ	always	ጥራይ	only
ወትሩ	always	በይኑ	alone
ወርትግ	always	ምናዳ	particularly, especially
ከቶ	never	አስታት	about, approximately
አበይ	where?	አቢሉ	about, approximately
ካበይ	from where?	ከመይ	how?

LESSON 31

Compound Tenses, ነበረ and ኩነ

The simple imperfect and the gerundive tenses are used with the verb ኣሎ *to be present*, to make compound tenses.

For the imperfect tense plus ኣሎ, see Lesson 19. The negative of this tense is made by the negative of the imperfect together with the corresponding form of ኣሎ, e.g. ኣይበልዕን ኣሎ *he is not eating*.

The gerundive with ኣሎ is used as the equivalent of the English present perfect.

    መጺኡ ኣሎ።   *He has come*
    ኣብ በረኻ ዕንጨይቲ ቆሪጸ ኣሎኹ። *I have cut wood in the wilderness.*

The verb ነበረ and its gerundive ነይሩ are used to express past time for both እዩ and ኣሎ. The conjugations are as follows:

	Singular		Plural	
3 m.	ነበረ	he was	ነበሩ	they were
f.	ነበረት	she was	ነበራ	they were
2 m.	ነበርካ	you were	ነበርኩም	you were
f.	ነበርኪ	you were	ነበርክን	you were
1 c.	ነበርኩ	I was	ነበርና	we were

	Singular		Plural	
3 m.	ነይሩ	he was	ነይሮም	they were
f.	ነይራ	she was	ነይረን	they were
2 m.	ኔርካ	you were	ኔርኩም	you were
f.	ኔርኪ	you were	ኔርክን	you were
1 c.	ነይረ	I was	ኔርና	we were

The gerundive plus the appropriate form of ነበረ or ነይሩ corresponds to the English past perfect. Literary usage may use the gerundive with ነበረ to form this tense, as in:

ደቁ መዛሙርቱ ግና ዚብላዕ ኪዕድጉ ናብ ከተማ ኸይዶም ነበሩ። *The disciples however had gone into the city to buy food.*

But the normal usage is ከይዶም ነይሮም *they had gone.*

To form the negative of this tense, the negative of the simple perfect plus ነበረ or ነይሩ is used.

አይከዱን ነበሩ or ነይሮም *They had not gone.*
ዮሃንስ ጌና ናብ ቤት ማእሰርቲ አይተአሰረን ነበረ። *For John had not yet been imprisoned.*

The imperfect with the corresponding form of ነበረ corresponds to the English past progressive or past imperfect.

ይበልዑ ነበሩ *They were eating*
or ይበልዑ ነይሮም. *They were eating*

To form the negative of this tense, the negative of the imperfect plus the corresponding form of ነበረ is used.

አይበልዑን ነበሩ *They were not eating*
አይበልዑን ነይሮም *They were not eating*

The verb ኮነ is used as follows:

1. To form the negative of the verb "to be" (see Lesson 7, አይኮንኩን etc.)

2. To form the future of the verb "to be," e.g. ሃብታም ኪኸውን እዩ *He will be rich.*

3.a. With the imperfect. The imperfect of ኮነ (ይከውን) is used to express doubt or probability. Note that ይከውን can be conjugated for person, gender, and number.

ናብ ዕዳጋ ይኽይድ ይከውን። *He may be on his way to market.*

To express present doubt or probability in the negative, the negative of the imperfect plus the imperfect ይከውን is used.

ናብ ገዛኡ ኣይመጽእን ይከውን። *I am probably not coming to his house.*

3.b. With the gerundive.

i. The imperfect ይከውን is used with the gerundive to express doubt in the past.

መጺኡ ይከውን። *He may have come.*

ii. With the gerundive interrogative, the imperfect ይከውን is used to ask a tactful question.

መጺኡዶ ኾን ይከውን፧ *Might he have come, possibly?*

LESSON 32

Verbal Adjectives and Nouns

Many adjectives and nouns are derived from verbs. That is, they are part of a system of words sharing the same root. The root is thought of as a set of radicals with a certain meaning.
For example, the word ማዕፆ *door*, like ዕፁው *closed*, is from the root ዐፀወ *close*. In this case the final ወ has been dropped or assimilated, as often happens with "weak" letters, but the common root can still be seen. There is some regularity in the way words are formed from the roots, and it is helpful to see this especially when learning vocabulary.

1. Verbal adjectives are passive participles, generally formed with the vowels 6-2-6. Thus from ሰበረ *break* is formed the adjective ስቡር *broken*, with its feminine ስብርት and plural ስቡራት. The form ስቡር has the vowels 6th form, 2d form, and 6th form, or 6-2-6. So also ክፉት *open*; ዕፁው *closed*; ግሩም *wonderful.*

2. Verbal nouns are formed in various ways. Two more or less regular patterns are:

   a. Nouns signifying the agent or the name of a profession are usually formed with the vowels 1-4-3, or sometimes 1-4-4 plus ይ.

ሰባሪ	ሰባሪት (f.)	ሰባርቲ (pl.)	*breaker*
ፈራዲ	*judge*		
ሐራዲ	*butcher*		
ዘዋሪ	*driver*		
ጸሐፊ or ጸሓፋይ			*writer* or *secretary*
ኣላሚ or ኣላማይ			*weaver*

b. Nouns signifying tools or instrumentality are often formed with መ plus 6-1-3, or መ plus 6-1-3 plus ት.

መጽረቢ	*plane* (carpenter's tool)
መድሃኒት	*medicine* (lit. *that saves* from disease)
መፈንቀሊ	*sledge-hammer* or *wedge*

Some of these nouns are formed with the vowels 6-1-6.

መንበር   *chair*

LESSON 33

Ordinal Numbers

The ordinal numbers are inflected for gender, and agree with the noun they modify.

masc.	fem.	
ቀዳማይ	ቀዳመይቲ	first
ካልአይ	ካልአይቲ	second
ሳልሳይ	ሳልሰይቲ	third
ራብዓይ	ራብዐይቲ	fourth
ሓምሻይ	ሓምሻይቲ	fifth
ሻድሻይ	ሻድሸይቲ	sixth
ሻብዓይ	ሻብዓይቲ	seventh
ሻምናይ	ሻምነይቲ	eighth
ታሽዓይ	ታሽዐይቲ	ninth
ዓስራይ	ዓስረይቲ	tenth

The ordinal numbers *eleventh* and higher are made by using the word መበል with the cardinal number.

መበል ዓስርተው ሓደ	eleventh
መበል ዓስርተው ክልተ	twelfth

Some common fractions are as follows.

ፍርቂ	one-half
ሲሶ	one-third
ርብዒ	one-fourth
ሕምሲት	one-fifth
ሓምሻይ እፍ or ሓምሻይ ኢድ	a fifth portion
ስምኒት	one-eighth
ዕስሪት	one-tenth

LESSON 34

Direct and Indirect Objects

The grammatical direct object of a verb can often be identified as the person or thing that receives the action of the verb. In some languages, like Latin and Greek, it is in a distinctive case (the accusative). In Tigrinya, it comes before the verb.

ካህን ጸሎት ወዲኡ። *The priest ended the prayer.*
እምብልታታቶም እናወቕዑ እቶም ሰብኡት ናብቲ ገዛ
አተዉ። *Playing their flutes, the men entered the house.*

The direct object of the verb may be introduced by ን prefixed, although this prefixed ን is not obligatory. When it is used, the verb will have a pronoun suffix that corresponds to the object. In the first sentence below, the suffixed ዎ is masculine singular, corresponding to the noun phrase, "his good friend." In effect, the object is expressed twice, once as noun and once as pronoun.

1. In any one nominal group, ን occurs only once.

    ነቲ ሕያዋይ ዓርኩ ርእየዮ። *I have seen his good friend.*

2. When there are several objects, ን can appear before each object, or it can appear only one time.

    ነቲ ሓለቓን ነቶም ወተሃደራትን ሓገዞም። *He helped the chief and the soldiers.*
    ንሓለቓን ወተሃደራትን ሓገዞም። *(the same)*

3. If the direct object is a pronoun, the verbal suffix alone can express it. However, a pronominal suffix can be added with ን , in the form ንአ . But the verb will still have its suffix. In effect, the object is expressed twice, both times as a pronoun.

    እቶም ቈልዑ ርኢዮኒ። *Those children saw me.*
    እቶም ቈልዑ ንኣይ ርኢዮኒ። *(the same)*

The indirect object is expressed by ን prefixed to the noun.

እቲ ጭቃ ንወትሃደራት ገንዘብ ሂብዎም። *The chief of the village gave money to the soldiers.*

If there are several indirect objects, ን may be used with each one, or only once.

ነቶም አወዳቱን ነተን አዋልዱን ገዛ ይህቦም። *He is giving the house to his sons and his daughters.*

ንአቦይን አደይን ተዛሪብዎም። *He spoke to my father and mother.*

In the second sentence, if the parents are addressed individually, it is better to use ን with each: ንአቦይን ንአደይን.

The direct object may be placed before the indirect, or vice-versa.

እዚ መጽሓፍ ንመምህር ሃቦ። *Give this book to the teacher.*
ንመምህር እዚ መጽሓፍ ሃቦ። *(the same)*

If the indirect object is a pronoun, the pronoun object suffixes of the verb may be employed. When ን. is used with a pronoun, pronoun suffixes of the type used with nouns are attached to the particle ንአ.

ኢሉኒ *He said to me.*
ንዓይ ሂቡኒ *He gave to me.*

The preposition ስ or ል

The preposition ስ or ል with a pronoun object suffix attached is used with verbs. It cannot introduce a noun. Its usual meaning is *on behalf of, for the benefit of.* With some verbs, it introduces an ordinary indirect object. In effect, this preposition ስ with its pronoun is like a Latin or Greek dative, which can be a "dative of advantage," a "dative of reference," or a "dative indirect object."

	Singular		Plural	
3 m.	–ሉ	*for him*	–ሎም	*for them*
f.	–ላ	*for her*	–ለን	*for them*
2 m.	–ልካ	*for you*	–ልኩም	*for you*
f.	–ልኪ	*for you*	–ልከን	*for you*
1 c.	–ለይ	*for me*	–ልና	*for us*

ማዕጾ ኸፊትዎ።   *He opened the door.*
ማዕጾ ኸፊቱሉ።   *He opened the door for him.*
ነቲ መጽሓፍ ባዕሉ ጸሒፍዎ።   *He wrote that book himself.*
መጽሓፍ ጸሒፉልና።   *He wrote a book for us.*
መስኪሩልካ።   *He testified on your behalf.*
ነቲ ኸልቢ ኣሰሮ።   *He tied the dog.*
ነቲ ኸልቢ ኣሲሩለይ።   *He tied the dog for me.*
ተፈቒዱልና።   *It is permitted for us.* (Latin *licet nobis*)
ኣምጽኣለይ።   *Bring [it] to me.*
መሊሱሎም።   *He gave them back.*
መሊሱሎም።   *He answered them.*

Some verbs, such as መለሰ *answer*, ሰገደ *worship*, ደንገጸ *pity*, use ን with the object expressed independently and ል with the corresponding object pronoun as it is suffixed to the verb.

ንኣምላኽ ሰገደሉ።   *He worshiped God.*
ፈራዲ ነቲ ሰራቒ ደንጊጹሉ።   *The judge pitied the thief.*

In compound tenses, the suffixes are always joined to the main verb and not to the auxiliary.

ነቲ ኸልቢ ይኣስሮ ነበረ።   *He was tying the dog.*

LESSON 35

Interrogatives

Questions can be asked with interrogative pronouns and adverbs.

እንታይ	what?
አበይ	where?
ካበይ	from where?
ናበይ	to where?
መኣስ	when?
መን	who?
ምስ መን	with whom?
ናይ መን	of whom, whose?
ንመን	to whom?
አየናይ	which?
ክንደይ	how many?
ከመይ	how?
ብምንታይ	how, by what means?
ንምንታይ	why, for what?
ስለምንታይ	why, for what reason?

If an interrogative word is not used, questions are formed with a special particle, ዶ. This is attached as a suffix to the appropriate word. But when it is attached to እዩ or ኣሎ, it is prefixed rather than suffixed, and does not have the 7th form vowel.

	with እዩ		with ኣሎ	
3 m.	ድዩ	ድዮም	ዶሎ	ዶሎው
f.	ድያ	ድየን	ዶላ	ዶለዋ
2 m.	ዲኻ	ዲኹም	ዶሎኻ	ዶሎኹም
f.	ዲኺ	ዲኽን	ዶሎኺ	ዶሎኽን
1 c.	ድየ	ዲና	ዶሎኹ	ዶሎና

The particle ዶ is used only once in a question.

ጽቡቕ ድዩ፣ ወይስ ሕማቕ እዩ፣ *Is it good or bad?*

When the answer expected is positive, ዶ is used with a negative verb (cf. Latin *nonne*).

ከልብን ተኹላን መብቆሎም ካብ ሓደ እዩ፣ ኣይኮነን፣ *The dog and the wolf are from the same species, aren't they?*

ከልብን ተኹላን መብቆሎም ሓደ ዶ ኣይኮነን፣ *Aren't the dog and the wolf from the same species?*

ዕባይ ከተማ ዶ ማሕረስ ይኽእል፣ *Do city boys know how to plow?*

ብዕራይ ዶ ይወልድ፣ *Can an ox have a calf?*

Questions are marked in speech by a rising intonation. The traditional written question mark ፧ (ስለስተ ነጥቢ *three dots*) has now largely been replaced by the mark " ? ," especially in handwriting.

LESSON 36

Causatives

The different stems of a verb, or themes (this is the term used by W. Leslau) are conjugations of the verb in which a regular transformation is applied through all the inflections of person, number, and so on. These transformations imply a regular effect on the meaning of the verb. For example, when a verb is systematically altered by prefixing the radical አ, the whole collection of new forms is the conjugation of the "causative stem" of the verb. The common meaning of these forms is generally the meaning of the root verb with the idea of causation added to it. Thus from ገበረ *do* is derived አገበረ *cause to do*.

The radical አ is a "weak" radical, and when it is added to another word its presence is not always obvious.

When አ is prefixed to a verb like ገደፈ *leave off*, which begins with a 6th form radical, the prefix and the radical make a single syllable that ends with the 6th form silent: አግደፈ *cause to leave off* (pronounced አግ – ደፈ).

When አ is prefixed to an inflected form of the verb beginning with a person marker like ይ or ት, the prefix causes the 6th form radical to become 1st form, and the radical አ of the prefix does not itself appear. ትባርክ *she blesses* plus አ becomes ታባርክ *she causes to bless*.

In type A verbs, and in family III.1, the first radical of the root remains in the 6th form.

Simple perfect	Imperfect	Gerundive	Jussive-imperative
አስበረ	ያስብር	አስብሮ	ያስብር
አጽሐፈ	ያጽሕፍ	አጽሒፎ	ያጽሕፍ

In type B and C verbs, the first radical keeps its original vowel.

Simple perfect	Imperfect	Gerundive	Jussive-imperative
አበደለ	የበድል	አበዲሉ	የብድል
አባረኸ	የባርኸ	አባሪኹ	የባርኸ

In all verbs, in the imperfect and jussive-imperative, the second and following radicals become 6th form.

In some verbs a letter, **ን** or **ም**, is added for the sake of pronunciation, between the causative prefix and the first radical of the root.

    ቀጥቀጠ   *pound,*   አንቀጥቀጠ   *tremble*

Notice the uses of the causative in the following examples.

ወጺኡ።	*He went out.*
ነታ ዱሙ አውጺእዎ።	*He caused the cat to go out.*
ትማሊ መጺኡ።	*He came yesterday.*
ትማሊ ነቲ ገንዘብ አምጺእዎ።	*He brought the money yesterday* (lit *caused the money to come*)
ነቲ ገንዘብ የምጽእ አሎ።	*He is bringing the money.*
ጽባሕ ነቲ ገንዘብ ኬምጽእ እዩ።	*He will bring the money tomorrow.*
ነቲ መጽሓፍ አብ ሰደቃ አቐምጦ።	*Put the book on the table.*

Some verbs are causative in form, but not causative in meaning.

    አመስገነ   *give thanks*
    አምለጠ   *escape*
    አለለየ   *recognize*

LESSON 37

Passives

To form the passive stem, the letter ተ is prefixed. However, in the imperfect, jussive, and infinitive, the ተ is assimilated by the first radical of the root and does not appear.

	Singular		Plural	
3 m.	ተሀረመ	he was struck	ተሀረሙ	they were struck
f.	ተሀረመት	she was struck	ተሀረግ	they were struck
2 m.	ተሀረምክ	you were struck	ተሀረምኩም	you were struck
f.	ተሀረምኪ	you were struck	ተሀረምከን	you were struck
1 c.	ተሀረምኩ	I was struck	ተሀረምን	we were struck

There is a relatively wide range of pronunciation of some forms of the passive.

In the simple perfect of type A verbs, when the third radical is a form other than 6th, the second radical usually becomes a 6th form. But sometimes an alternate spelling with the 1st form exists. Thus ተሰብረ and ተሰበረ are equivalent. The meaning is *it was broken*, a passive from ሰበረ *break*.

In type A and B verbs, in the imperfect, the first radical becomes 6th form, and the second remains 1st form. For example, the simple imperfect እምኒ ገለ ይሰብር *the stone was breaking something*, becomes in the passive እምኒ ይስበር *the stone was being broken*. The ሰ becomes ስ but በ remains በ.

When the passive is formed of the simple perfect of family III.1, the first radical becomes 4th form and the second radical becomes 6th form. Thus the simple perfect ጸሐፈ *he wrote* becomes ተጻሕፈ *it was written.* For the imperfect passive of family III.1, the second radical becomes 1st form. Thus ይጽሕፍ *he was writing* when made passive is ይጻሕፍ *it was being written.* For the jussive-imperative passive of family III.1, the first radical becomes 1st form. Thus ይጽሐፍ *let him write* becomes the passive ይጻሐፍ *let it be written.*

The passive is used as a regular passive, as a reflexive (the Greek "middle"), and as a deponent. A deponent verb is one that is "passive in form but active in meaning," like Latin *hortor* "I exhort," not "I am exhorted." Tigrinya examples are:

እቲ ወዲ ተሃሪሙ።	*The boy was hit.* (passive)
እቲ ሽሓኒ ተሓጺቡ።	*The plate has been washed.* (passive)
ተሓጺባ።	*She washed herself.* (reflexive, or "middle")
ተዛረበ	*speak* (deponent)
ተጻወተ	*play* (deponent)
ተመነየ	*desire, covet* (deponent)

LESSON 38

Relatives

Introduction

Relative clauses in English are usually introduced by the relative pronouns, *who, which, that,* and so on. "The letter you wrote," and "the letter that you wrote," amount to the same thing, but the second uses the relative pronoun "that" to introduce the clause "you wrote." Tigrinya does not use a separate word for this function. Instead, the simple perfect or imperfect of the verb is inflected by prefixing ዝ or እ to it.

    መልእኽቲ ጽሒፍካ   *You wrote a letter.*
    ዝጽሓፍካዮ መልእኽቲ   *the letter [that] you wrote [it]*

The second phrase might be translated *the you-wrote-it letter,* in order to display the fact that the modifying or defining clause in Tigrinya is one word, not several words as in English. It also illustrates how the Tigrinya word is something like a participle. It can be made into a substantive by using an article.

    ዚመጽእ ሰሙን   *the coming week*
    እቲ ዚመጽእ መን እዩ!   *That person coming, who is it?*

Formation of the Relative

In general, the relative prefix is ዝ . Its vowel can be modified by the radicals that follow it. However, when the verb begins with the personal markers ት or ን , the prefix is እ rather than ዝ . Further details about these prefixes follow.

ዝ is prefixed to the simple perfect or imperfect.

    ገበረ *he did*   ዝገበረ *that did*
    ይገብር *he is doing*   ዚገብር *that is doing*

እ is used in front of the personal markers ት and ን. The person markers are doubled when the relative is prefixed.

እንገብር   *we who are doing*
እትገብር   *you who are doing*

እ (rarely ዝ) is used in front of the passive prefix ተ.

እተገብረ   *that was done*
እተዳለወ   *that was made ready; prepared*
እተጻሕፈ መልእኽቲ   *a letter that was written*

When ዝ precedes እ, the first person singular marker, the marker is dropped and only ዝ appears.

እሰምዕ   *I am listening*   **ዝሰምዕ**   *I who listen*

When ዝ precedes ይ, the combination becomes ዚ.

ይገብር   *he is doing*   **ዚገብር**   *that is doing*

ዝ with አሎ makes ዘሎ, and so forth.

እምነት ዘላቶ   *the one who has faith*

A negative verb in the indicative begins with አይ and ends with ን. With the relative, the verb begins with ዘይ and the suffix ን is not used.

እቲ ዘይገበሮ ወዲ   *the boy who did not do it*

When ዝ precedes እ, from the causative, the combination becomes ዘ.

Usage

When the relative clause is an adjective clause, it comes before the noun. For example,

እታ ዝመጸት ጓል ሳራ እያ። *The girl who came is Sarah.*

ነታ ትማሊ ዝመጸት ጓል ጸዋዓያ። *Call the girl who came yesterday* (lit *To the yesterday arrived girl, call her*. This sentence would also be correct without the preposition **ን**, that is, with **እታ** instead of **ነታ**.)

When the relative clause is a noun clause, it replaces the noun in the sentence order.

ናብ ከረን ደይቡ ድማ፡ ንዝደለዮም ጸውዔ፡ ናብኡ ኸአ መጹ። *He went up into a mountain and called whom he would, and they came to him.*

Points of construction

The verb in the relative clause has the usual object suffixes, direct and indirect.

እቲ እትርእዮ ዘሎኻ ሰብ ኩናማ እዩ። *The man whom you see is from Kunama.*
እቲ ዝገበርካለይ ብዙሕ እዩ። *What you have done for me is much.*

When the semantic relationship of the verb in a relative clause to the noun it modifies is indirect, the preposition **ል** and the third person pronouns may be used for the suffixes of the verb. (The suffixes would be **–ሎ –ላ –ሎም –ለን**)

እታ እትጻወተላ ዘሎኻ ኩዕሶ ከባብ ኣይኮነትን። *The ball you are playing with isn't round.* The instrumental "with" accounts for the preposition **ል** in **እትጻወተላ**.
እቲ ዝሓደርናሉ ሆተል ናይ ተስፋይ እዩ። *The hotel in which we spent the night belongs to Tesfai.*
ብታ እተወለድኩላ ዓመት ብርቱዕ ዝናም ዘነመ። *There were heavy rains in the year that I was born.*

There are some verbs, such as ሰፈረ *stay a while*, and አሎ *be present*, that might seem to require the preposition ል but which do not use it. They use the direct object suffix.

> እቲ ዝሰፈርናዮ ዓዲ ሃሩር እዩ። *The village we stopped in is hot.*
> እቲ ዘሎናዮ ገዛ ገፊሕ እዩ። *The house we are in is large.*

If the verb in the relative clause has a direct object marked with the prefix ን, the verb does not take an object suffix.

> እታ ንዋና-ጸሓፊ ዝረአየት ሰበይቲ ሓብተይ እያ። *The woman who has seen the First Secretary is my sister.* (Note that the form ዝረአየት is used, rather than ዝረአየቶ.)

The relative construction is used often with the verb "to be." Depending on the emphasis, either the relative or the verb can be last.

> እቲ ዝኸደ ሓወይ እዩ። *The person who just left is my brother.*
> ሓወይ እዩ ዝኸደ። *My brother is the one that went.*

In a question, the word order is often the relative, the interrogative, and then the verb "to be."

> እዚ ዝገበረ መን እዩ ፧ *The one who did this is who?*

The relative with a negative verb and the word እኳ is used to mean "not even" in a defensive sense.

> ንስኻ ሰቢርካዮ። እዋይ ዘይሓዝክዎ እኳ። *You broke it! —What! I haven't even touched it!*

LESSON 39

Comparatives and Superlatives

The comparative is expressed by using the verb in the imperfect with **ካብ**.

ጸጋ ካብ ሓብታ ትነውሕ። *Tsega is taller than her sister.*

ካብታ ናይ ትማሊ እቲ ሎሚ ዝኾዓትናዮ ይበዝሕ። *We have dug more ground today than yesterday* (lit *From that of yesterday what today we have dug is more*).

ምድሪ ካብ ጸሓይ ትንእስ። *The earth is smaller than the sun.*

Question sentences and negative sentences using the comparative follow the rule except in such sentences as: "Which is smaller, the sun or the earth?"

አየናይ ይንእስ፣ ጸሓይ'ዶ ወይስ ምድሪ፧ *Which is smaller, the sun or the earth?*

Note that there is no **ካብ**; only the verb is used.

The superlative in Tigrinya is expressed by the use of a relative clause.

እዚ እቲ ዝነውሐ ገመድ እዩ። *This is the longest rope.*

እቲ ዝበለጸ ወዲ እዚ እዩ። *This is the best boy.*

እዚኣ እታ ዝበለጸት ጓል እያ። *This is the best girl.*

LESSON 40

Coordinate Conjunctions and Interjections

A coordinate conjunction is a word that like "and," connects two words, phrases, or clauses, that are grammatically or logically parallel. By way of comparison, a subordinate conjunction is a word like "since," which connects two clauses but represents one of them as an explanation or cause of the other. The main clause is stated and the other clause is subordinated to it. Subordinate conjunctions are treated in the next lesson.

1. **ን** *and* is the most common coordinate conjunction. It is placed at the end of each word that is to be joined. Thus in any use it must occur two or more times.

    ሰደቻን ወንበርን አምጽእ። *Bring a table and chair.*

    መጽሓፍካን ጥራዝካን ውሰድ። *Take your book and your exercise book.*

2. **ውን** *and* (**እውን** after a word ending in a vowel)

    a. **ውን** *and* is used to bind two clauses together, and is placed after the word which is to be emphasized.

    ናብ ቤት ትምህርቲ ከይዱ አብሉ እውን ኩዕሶ ተጻዊቱ። *He went to school and there he played ball.*

    ናብ ቤት ትምህርቲ ከይዱ ኩዕሶ እውን ተጻዊቱ። *He went to school and played ball.*

    b. It is sometimes used to mean "then."

    ንጽብሒቱ እውን ናብ ገዛ ዋና እተን ከብቲ ከይዱ። *Then, the next day, he went to the house of the owner of the cattle.*

    c. It is used to mean "also"

    ፈረሰይ'ውን ሞይቱ፡ *My horse also is dead.*

3. **ከአ** or **ኸአ**   *and, also*

   አነ ኸአ ጐይታይ፥ ክሳዕ መኣዝ፤   *And I said, "Lord, until when?"*

4. **ድማ**   *and, also*

   ንሱ ድማ ከተማታት ክሳዕ ዝባድማ በለ።   *And he said, "Until the cities are wasted." (Isaiah 6:11)*

   When used together in a compound sentence, **ከአ** and **ድማ** mean *and*. Usually **ከአ** precedes and **ድማ** follows.

5. **ስጋብ**   *until* (also **ክሳዕ**). This word is used only with the simple imperfect tense.

6. **ወይ**   *or*

   ብእግሪ ወይ ብበቕሊ ከትከዱ ትኽእሉ ኢኹም።   *You can go by foot or by mule.*

7. **ኩን**   *either* (**ኩን ... ኩን**   *whether ... or*). Often in speech only the initial **ኩን** is used.

   ንያዕቆብ ጽቡቕ ኩን ክፉእ ከይትዛረቦ ተጠንቀቕ በሎ።
   Take care you speak not either good or bad to Jacob. (Genesis 31:24)

   ጳውሎስ ወይ አጵሎስ፥ ኬፋ ኩን ዓለም ኩነት፥ ህይወት ኩነት ሞት ኩን፥   *Whether Paul or Apollos, Cephas, the world, or life, or death* (1 Cor 3:22).

8. **አሸንኣይ'ዶ ... ውን**   *not only ... but also*

   አሸንኣይ አራዊት ሰብ'ውን ጨካን እዩ።   *Not only wild animals but people also are cruel.*

9. **ጊና** or **ግን**   *but* (adversative)

   እዚ ወደይ እዩ፥ እቲ ግን ወዲ ሐወይ እዩ።   *This is my son, but that is my brother's son.*

10. **እምበር** *but*

   a. **እምበር** is used mainly with a negative comparison. The word order of the sentence is typically (1) the positive statement, (2) **እምበር**, and (3) the negative statement. The verb is not used in the positive statement if it is the same as the verb of the negative statement.

   እቶም ፈሪሳውያን ክብሪ ሰብ እምበር፣ ንኽብሪ እምላኽ ኣይደለዩን። *The Pharisees (desired) the glory of men, but did not desire the glory of God.*

   b. It is used as a mild adversative, as in a resumptive sense.

   እምበር'ዶ ገንዘብ ኣለዎ፧ *But does he have money?*

   c. It is used to express something unexpected.

   ንሱ እምበር መጺኡ። *But instead he came* (although he was not expected to come).

11. **እምበአር** *therefore, so.* The rhetorical particle **ሲ** is often used with **እምበአር**.

   እምበአርሲ፣ ኣብርሃም ኣቦና፣ ብስጋ እንታይ ረኺቡ፣ ክንብል ኢና፧ *What shall we say that Abraham our father in the flesh has found?* (Romans 4:1)

12. **ደአ** *better, rather, in preference to, sooner*

   ነዛ ፈረስ እዚ እሰር ደአ። *Better tie this horse.*
   እዚ ደአ ክወስድ። *I had rather take this one.*

13. **ጋዳ** *please* (also, but rarely, **ኩታ**)

   ምሃረና ጋዳ። *Please teach us.*

14. **እም** *therefore, in consequence* (always postpositive—i.e. not the first word in its phrase)

ሎሚ ክኸይድ እየ እሞ፣ ነዚ ስራሕ ባዕልኻ ግበር። *I will go today, therefore you do this work yourself.*

15. **እኳ**   *not even, even*

    ሓንቲ ሳንቲም እኳ የብለይን። *I don't have even one cent.*

    እቲ ካብ ከተማኹም ዝለገባና ተጉን እኳ ንንግፈልኩም እሎና። *We are wiping off against you even the dust of your cities that sticks to us.* (Luke 10:11)

16. **ደጊም**   *therefore*

    ካብ ንግሆ ክሳዕ ምሸት ሰሪሕና እሞ፣ ደጊም ንዕረፍ። *We worked from morning till evening, so let us rest.*

17. **ስለምንታይ**   *why?*

    ስለምንታይ ናብ አስመራ ኬድካ፤ *Why have you gone to Asmara?*

18. **ብዘተረፈ**   *finally* (lit *for what remains*.). This word signals the conclusion of a discourse).

    ብዘተረፈ ዋጋ እዚ መጽሓፍ'ዚ ሕሱር እዩ። *And finally, the price of this book is cheap.*

    ብዘተረፈስ አሕዋተይ፣ ብጎይታ ተሓጎሱ። *Finally, my brothers, rejoice in the Lord.* (Philippians 3:1)

19. **ማለት**   *that is to say, that means*

    እቶም ደቂ፣ ማለት ተክለን አብርሃምን ናብ ሩባ ወረዱ። *The children, that is Tekle and Abraham, went down to the river.*

List of coordinate conjunctions and interjections

1. **ን ን**   *and*
2. **ውን**   *and* (**እውን** after a word ending in a vowel)
3. **ከኣ**   *and, also*
4. **ድማ**   *and, also*
5. **ስጋብ**   *until* (also **ክሳዕ**) only with s.impf. tense.
6. **ወይ**   *or*
7. **ኮነ**   *either* (**ኮነ** ... **ኮነ** *whether ... or*)
8. **አሽንኳይ'ዶ ... ውን**   *not only ... but also*
9. **ኔሩ** or **ግን**   *but* (adversative)
10. **እምበር**   *but*
    a. mainly with a negative comparison.
    b. as a mild adversative, as in a resumptive sense—returning to a topic in the course of discussion.
    c. to express something unexpected.
11. **እምበኣር**   *therefore, so.*
12. **ደኣ**   *better, rather, in preference to, sooner*
13. **ግዳ**   *please* (also, but rarely, **ኮታ**)
14. **እሞ**   *therefore, in consequence* (always post-positive, that is, occuring after the first word of a phrase)
15. **እኳ**   *not even, even*
16. **ደጊም**   *therefore*
17. **ስለምንታይ**   *why?*
18. **ብዘተረፈ**   *finally* (lit *for what remains.*).
19. **ማለት**   *that is to say, that means*

LESSON 41

Subordinate Conjunctions

Subordinate conjunctions join two elements, but not in parallel. The two elements that are joined may differ grammatically to a greater or lesser extent, along with the logical and syntactic subordination. This is true in English and in other languages. For example, in "She *went* to the river and *washed* her clothes," the verbs "went" and "washed" are parallel and are joined by means of the coordinate conjunction "and." But when a relation of time, purpose, or result is expressed, the verbs may no longer be grammatically parallel. Thus, "She *went* to the river *to wash* her clothes," or, "After *going* to the river, she *washed* her clothes" no longer use the two simple past tenses "went" and "washed." The following paragraphs give examples of such constructions in Tigrinya.

1. ስጋብ *until, up to, as far as* (also spelled ስጋዕ. An equivalent word less widely used is ክሳዕ or ክሳብ). The conjunction is followed by ዝ with the simple imperfect.

    ክጾወት መሰል የብሉን ስጋብ ስርሑ ዝውድእ። *He has no right to amuse himself until he has finished his work.*

2.a. ካብ or እንካብ *than*. With ዝ and the simple imperfect.

    ከዘውር እፈቱ ካብ ንስራሕ ምኻድ። *I like to go for a walk better than to work.*

2.b. ካብ *since, because*. With the simple perfect, or with ዝ and the simple imperfect.

    ካብ በልካንስ እያእምነካን እየ። *Since you said that to me, I don't believe you.* The suffix ስ of በልካኒ is a rhetorical addition.

    እዚ ካብ በልካኒ አይአምኖን እየ። *Since you said this to me, I don't believe him.* The conjunctions እም and ስለ

are more common than **ካብ** in this type of construction.

እዚ ስለ ዝብለኒ *because he says this to me ...*
እዚ ኢሉኒ እዮ'ሞ፣ ስለዚ *well, he said this to me, and so ...*

3. **ከ..., ከ...** with the simple imperfect and **ኣሎ** : *while*. The simple imperfect with **ኣሎ** is conjugated normally, but the particle **ከ** is prefixed to both verb elements. This construction is for an action that is simultaneous with the main verb.

   ከበልዕ ከለኹ ርእዩኒ። *While I was eating he saw me.*

4.a. **ከይ** with the simple imperfect is a negative purpose construction : *lest*. The construction is also used with the verbs **ፈርሀ** *fear* and **ጠርጠረ** *doubt*.

   ከይስበር ተጠንቀቕ *Be careful that it doesn't break.*
   ከይወድቕ እፈርህ *I'm afraid that he might fall.*

4.b. **ከይ** with the simple perfect expresses an unfulfilled circumstance.

   ከይነገረኒ መጺኡ *He came without letting me know.*
   ከይከደ ጸውዓዮ *Before he goes, call him.*

5. **ምእንቲ** *in order to, for the purpose of.*

   ምሕረት ክዳውንታ ምእንቲ ክትሓጽብ ናብቲ ሩባ ወረደ። *Meheret went to the river to wash her clothes.*

6. **ስለ** *because* (answers a question "why"), with **ዝ** and the simple perfect.

   በሊዑ ስለ ዝነበረ *because he had eaten*

7. **ከም** *that*, with **ዝ** and the simple perfect or imperfect, is a form for indirect speech. It is used after verbs of perception.

> **ከም ዝመጸ እፈልጥ።** *I know that he came.*
>
> **ከም ዝመጽእ እፈልጥ።** *I know that he will come.*

8. **ምንም እኳ ... እንተ**, or **ሽሕ እኳ ... እንተ**, with the simple perfect : *even if, although*. **እንተ** comes before the verb.

> **ምንም እኳ ሃብታም እንተ ኩንኩ** *even if I were rich*
>
> **ምንም እኳ ዕዳኻ እንተከፈልካ** *even if you pay your debts*

9. **እንተ** with **ዝ** and the simple imperfect is used to express a wish. A wish can also be expressed with the jussive.

> **ዘእክል ገንዘብ እንተዝሀልወኒ** *If I only had enough money!*
>
> **ኣየ ንሱ እንተ ዚመጽእ** *If he could only come!*
>
> **የምጽእለይ** *I wish he would come* (the jussive; lit *may he (God) make him come for me*)

10. **ኣብ ክንዲ** *instead of* can be followed by a relative clause.

> **ኣብ ክንዲ ዚዛረብ ትም ይበል።** *Instead of speaking, let him keep silent.*

11. **ምስ** *with*. Used with the simple perfect.

> **ንሱ ምስ መጸ፡ ኩሉ ኺነግረና እዩ።** *When he comes, he will tell us all things.*
>
> **ንሱ ምስ መጸ ኩሉ ነገሮም።** *When he came he told them everything.*

12. **እና** with the simple perfect is used when two actions take place at the same time and have the same subject : *while*.

እናሰሐቐ ወጸኣ *He went out laughing.*

Summary chart of subordinate conjuctions

	conjunction	translation	construction
1.	ሲጋብ or ክሳዕ	until	ዝ + s.impf.
2.a.	ካብ or እንካብ	than	ዝ + s.impf.
2.b.	ካብ	since, because	ዝ + s.impf. or pf.
3.	ከ , ከ	while	ከ with verb and ኣሎ
4.a.	ከይ	lest	s.impf.
4.b.	ከይ	without, before	s.pf.
5.	ምእንቲ	in order to	ከ + s.impf.
6.	ስለ	because	ዝ + s.pf.
7.	ከም	that	ዝ + s.impf. or pf.
8.	ምንም እኳ ... እንተ or ሽሕ እኳ ... እንተ	even if	s.pf.
9.	እንተ	expresses a wish	ዝ + s.impf.
10.	ኣብ ክንዲ	instead of	ዝ + s.impf.
11.	ምስ	when	s.pf.
12.	እና	while	s.pf.

LESSON 42

Reciprocals and Frequentatives

The reciprocal and frequentative systems or themes are formed by making an internal change to the verb instead of by adding a prefix or suffix.

The *reciprocal* system can be made from the passive system, as well as from the causative system, by giving the third or last radical of the verb a 4th form vowel. For a typical three-radical verb, this would be the first radical, and the root will start with a 4th form vowel.

> ዮሃንስን ተስፋይን ንሓድሕዶም ትሳሓቑ። *Yohannes and Tesfai laughed at each other.*
>
> ንሕድሕና እንተ ተፈቒርና፡ አምላኽ አባና ይነብር። *If we love one another, God remains in us.*

Some verbs, such as ባረኸ *bless*, ናፈቐ *long for*, and ላጸየ *shave*, have their normal conjugation in this form, except for the nounal infinitive, which is plain, and the frequentative, which is explained below. A chart gives the conjugation of ናፈቐ.

The *frequentative* system is formed by repeating the second-to-last radical of the verb. The first of the two repeated radicals is written with the 4th form vowel. The frequentatives can be formed from the active, the passive, and the causative stems. The basic meaning of the frequentative is repeated or continuous action.

> እንዳ ጻዓርና ድርቂ ግን ይመላለሰና እሎ። *Despite our efforts, famine keeps coming back.*
>
> እዚ አቑጽልቲ ኩሉ ጊዜ ይንቀሳቐስ ፋላ ንፋስ እንተ ዘሓለ። *The leaves keep waving even when the wind is low.*

Lesson 42 – Internal Stem Change

to long for	perfect	imperfect	imperative-jussive	gerundive	future
I –1 sing.	ናፈቅኩ	እናፍቃለሁ	እናፍቅ	ናፍቄ	ከናፍቃለሁ
you –1 pl.	ናፈቅን	እንናፍቃለን	እንናፍቅ	ናፍቀን	እንናፍቃለን
we –1 pl.	ናፈቅህ	ትናፍቃለህ	ናፍቅ	ናፍቀህ	ትናፍቃለህ
you –2 m.sg.	ናፈቅሽ	ትናፍቂአለሽ	ናፍቂ	ናፍቀሽ	ትናፍቂአለሽ
you –2 f.sg.	ናፈቃችሁ	ትናፍቃላችሁ	ናፍቁ	ናፍቃችሁም	ትናፍቃላችሁ
you –2 m.pl.	ናፈቃችን	ይናፍቃል	ይናፍቅ	ናፍቆ	ይናፍቃል
you –2 f.pl.	ናፈቀች	ትናፍቃለች	ትናፍቅ	ናፍቃ	ትናፍቃለች
he –3 m.sg.	ናፈቁ	ይናፍቃሉ	ይናፍቁ	ናፍቀው'ና'ቃው	ይናፍቃሉ
she –3 f.sg.	ናፈቁ	ይናፍቃሉ	ይናፍቁ	ናፍቀው	ይናፍቃሉ
they –3 m.pl.					
they –3 f.pl.					
negatives	አይናፈቅን	አይናፍቅን	አይናፍቅ	አይናፍቁ	አይናፍቃሁ

103

LESSON 43

በለ Verb

The verb በለ was originally በሀለ. Its basic meaning is "say," but it has many idiomatic uses. Some of its tenses are given below, followed by a number of uses. In many of these uses, በለ means something like *to act* in a way determined by the context. It resembles an English "helping verb" like "to do," whose meaning comes from the verb it accompanies. Note paragraphs 3, 4, and 6 below.

በለ	perfect
ቢሉ or ኢሉ	gerundive
ይብል	imperfect
በል	imperative

1. በለ can be added before or after the imperative of another verb, as an exclamation. This use is similar to the use of "Well, then," in English.

    በል ኪድ   *Well then, go.*
    ንዓና በል   *Let's go* (i.e. *accompany me*).

2. The gerundive form ኢሉ, or less commonly ቢሉ, is used at the end of a direct quotation. The main verb follows, specifying the kind of speech act that has just been related: speaking, asking, commanding, and so forth.

    የሱስ ንደቀ መዛሙርቱ ስዓቡኒ ኢሉ አዘዞም።   lit *Jesus said to his disciples "Follow me"— he commanded them.*

This example could be translated, *Jesus commanded his disciples to follow him,* or, *Jesus commanded his disciples, "Follow me."*

3. It can express purpose.

ከዳውንቲ ክትዕድግ ኢላ፡ ናብ ድኳን አትያ። *She went into the shop to buy clothes.*

4. It may be conjugated and used adverbially.

ተሎ ኢሉ መጸ። *He came quickly.*

5. It is used like English "say," "oh," to get attention.

በል ሓብትይ *Oh, Sister . . .*

6. In the form of the causative gerundive አቢሉ , it means *by, across, near, through, about, approximately,* etc.

ብከረን አቢሉ መጺኡ። *He came, passing through Keren.*
ሰዓት ሰለስተ አቢለ ክመጽአካ እየ። *I'll come to you about three o'clock.*

7. It is used alone as an exclamation, meaning *to act on something*. What specific action is in mind varies according to context. Thus it is used to encourage someone playing soccer, with the ball as a feminine singular object suffix: በላ *kick it!*

8. በል is commonly used with certain invariable forms that are not conjugated. Prepositions if any come between በል and the invariable. Prefixes and suffixes are attached to በል . In this usage, በል is fully conjugated in its active and causative forms. It does not use the passive.

ሐፍ በል	Stand up
ኮፍ በል	Sit down
ሱቕ በል	Be quiet
ጸው በል	Get lost
ቀስ በል	Slow down, Be careful

ጽን በል	Listen carefully
ጋው በል	Be loud
ደው በል	Stop
ፋሕ በል	Spread out, Scatter
ጠጎም በል	Taste it

9. An intensive force may be given to some verbs by putting all radicals in the 6th form, and using በለ in a manner similar to the manner just noted (paragraph 8).

ግልጽ ኢሉ	He looked around
ፍግም ኢሉ	He bowed down
ሀዲሙ	He ran away
ህድም ኢሉ	He ran away as fast as he could
ቀርቡ	He came near, is near to finishing
ቅርብ ኢሉ	He sneaked up

LESSON 44

Direct Speech

Often in Tigrinya direct speech is used where English uses indirect speech. Thus *Jesus told his disciples to follow him,* would be said in Tigrinya: የሱስ ንደቂ መዛሙርቱ፤ ስዓቡኒ፣ በሎም።

The direct quotation is closed with the verb በለ. Following it, another verb such as ጨደሩ *he shouted* or መለሰ *he answered* will make the action more specific. In this case the general act of saying is conveyed by በለ, and the content or purpose of what is said is conveyed by the second verb. The two verbs can occur together with no conjunction: ኢሉ መለሰ *he said he answered.* The effect in English is one of repetition. One might compare the language of the Authorized Version, "answered and said," "called and said," and so forth. Such phrases occur because the Hebrew uses two verbs where only one is necessary in English, but the translators imitated the Hebrew syntax and included both verbs.

In written Tigrinya, the quotation can be marked off with punctuation. Preceding is ፤ and following is ። . The usual word order is: first the subject; then the preposition ን and the person spoken to; next the words quoted, with the marks of punctuation; finally the verb phrase. In the verb phrase, በለ comes first; next, any modifiers to the second verb; last, the second verb. In the following example (John 3:3), the translation follows this word order rather than what English requires.

የሱስ ንኒቀዲሞስ፤ ካብ ላዕሊ እንተ ዘይተወልደ ንመንግስቲ እምላኽ ክርእያ ዚኽእል ከም ዘየሎ፣ ብሓቂ ብሓቂ እብለካ አሎኹ፣ ኢሉ መለሰሉ።

Jesus to Nicodemus: "If you are not born from above, that you will not be able to see the kingdom of God, in all truth I am telling you," he said, he answered him.

LESSON 45

Indirect Discourse

Verbs of saying, telling, reporting, commanding, and so on, that are not followed by a direct quotation, are generally followed by a subordinate clause specifying what was said. In English, the relative pronoun of the subordinate clause is often omitted. The following are grammatical examples in English:

1. Direct quotation. *She says, "Cactuses won't grow in Italy."*
2. Indirect. *She says that cactuses won't grow in Italy.*
3. Indirect, omitting the relative pronoun "that": *She says cactuses won't grow in Italy.*

The form of an English sentence may not correspond exactly to the form of a Tigrinya sentence that expresses the same idea. The following examples cover subordinate constructions with verbs of saying, telling, knowing, thinking, and the like.

Statements in indirect discourse

A. In the present.

ቶማስ እኹል ጨው ከምዘሎ እናፈለጠ ንምንታይ ዝያዳ ይሓይ፧ *Tom knows we have enough salt, why is he asking about more?*

B. Action in the future. The adverbial infinitive (ከ + imperfect) is used.

ሽዑ የሱስ ከይበኽዩ አዘዞም። *Then Jesus commanded them not to cry.*

C. Relative clause construction for the thing said.

ንጉስ አከአብ፡ እቲ ኢልያስ ዝገበሮ ኩሉ ንኢዛቤል ነገራ። *King Ahab told Jezebel all that Elijah had done.*

D. Past tense. ከም ዝ + simple perfect is used.

ሳሙኤል ኣብ ከንዲ ሽኮር ጨው ናብ ሻሂኡ ከምዝገበረሉ ንሓብቱ ነገራ። *Samuel told his sister how he had put salt instead of sugar in the tea.*

E. For the English construction "of" with a possessive and a gerund, use the nounal infinitive.

ምምጽኡ ኣይሰማዕኩን። *I didn't hear of his coming.*

Questions in indirect discourse

A. Indirect questions introduced by "if" or "whether," and thus admitting possibility or doubt, are expressed as follows.

1. For present or incomplete action, use ዝ with the simple imperfect እንተኾነ.

   ጸባሕ ምሳይ ዝኸይድ እንተኾነ ጠይቆ፤ *Ask him whether he will accompany me tomorrow.*

2. For past or complete action, use the gerundive and እንተኾነ.

   ትማሊ መጺኡ እንተኾነ ጠይቆ፤ *Ask him if he came yesterday.*

B. Indirect questions introduced by an interrogative word are expresssed as follows.

1. For present or incomplete action, use the interrogative, ከምዝ, and the simple imperfect.

   ጽባሕ ኣበይ ከምዝምስሑ ተፈልጥ'ዶ፤ *Do you know where they will take lunch tomorrow?*

ንግስቲ ቀመም አበይ ከምዝረከበቶ አይፈልጥን። *I don't know where Negisty found the spice.*

2. For past or complete action, use the interrogative, **ከምዝ**, and the simple perfect.

አበይ ከምዝሰርሑ ትፈልጥ'ዶ፧ *Do you know where they worked?*

አበይ ከምዝተወልደት አይፈልጥን። *I don't know where she was born.*

LESSON 46

Defective and Irregular Verbs

Defective

The verbs **እየ** and **አሎ** are called defective verbs because they do not have forms in all tenses. The forms they lack are supplied from other verbs.

እየ

	forms	comments
simple imperfect	እየ	
simple impf. negative	አይኮነን	negative of ኮነ
simple perfect	ነበረ	
gerundive	ኪነሩ or ነይሩ	
future	ኪኸውን	future of ኮነ
imperative-jussive	ኩን , ይኹን	imptv-juss. of ኮነ
nounal infinitive	ምኻን	from ኮነ

አሎ

	forms	comments
simple imperfect	አሎ	
simple impf. negative	የሉን	or የልቦን (unconjugated)
simple perfect	ነበረ	
gerundive	ኪነሩ or ነይሩ	
future	ከህሉ እየ	from ሀለወ
imperative-jussive	ይህሉ	expressing uncertainty
nounal infinitive	ምህላው	from ሀለወ

Example for the imperative-jussive of **እየ**:
በእምሮ ሰብኡት ኩኑ፥ ብክፍአት ደአ ሕጻናት ኩኑ እምበር፥ ብዛዕባ ስነ ፍልጠት ግና፥ ቄልዑ አይትኹኑ። *In mind, be men; in evil, be infants; but in understanding do not be children* (1 Cor 14:20).

Irregular

Three important irregular verbs are ሀበ , ሕዘ , and በለ . In their conjugations, many forms can be explained as abbreviations of forms from the conjugation of a more regular, triconsonantal verb.

1. ሀበ means *give*. It is derived from ወሃበ , and in some forms the ወ appears.

2. ሕዘ means *hold*. It is probably derived from *ተሕዘ . The initial radical appears in some stems with an internal change.

3. በለ means *say*. It is derived from በሀለ , and in some forms the ሀ appears.

See the following chart for a synopsis of these verbs.

Repeated final radicals

In Type A verbs, that is, verbs without doubling of the second-to-last radical, a consonant may be dropped from the spelling under certain circumstances. This happens when a 6th form radical with its vowel silent or final comes before another radical of the same consonant. The 6th form radical is dropped, and the two consonants are written as one. However, in pronunciation there will still be some differentiation of such a consonant. This contraction of spelling does not apply to Type B verbs, where the middle radical is geminated (doubled).

type A		type B, geminated	
ሐተተ	ask	አዘዘ	command
ይሐቱ፥	they are asking	ይአዝዙ	they are commanding
ተሐተ	he was asked	ተአዘዘ	he is commanded

Lesson 46: Give, Hold, Say

Irregular verbs	simple perfect	simple imperfect	gerundive	imperative-jussive	agent	nounal infinitive
give, active	ሰጰ	ይሀብ	ሀቦ-	ሀብ – ይሀብ	ወሃቢ	ምሃብ
be given, pass.	ተወሀበ	ይወሀብ	ተወሂቡ-	ይወሀብ	ተወሃቢ	ምሃብ or ምውሃብ
hold, active	ሐዘ	ይሕዝ	ሒዞ-	ሕዝ – ይሕዝ	ሐዚ	ምሕዝ
be held, pass.	ተሐዘ	ይትሐዝ	ይሕዝ	ትታሐዙ	ተትሐዚ	ምትሐዝ
say, active	በለ	ይብል	ኢሎ-	በል	በሃሊ	ይበሎ
be said, passive	ተብህለ	ይብሀል	ተብህሎ-	ትብሀል	ተብሃሊ	ምብሀሎ

LESSON 47
Impersonal Verbs

Impersonal verbs are used in the 3d person singular, of whatever tense, like English "it is necessary," "it was necessary," "it will be necessary." Tigrinya has no neuter ("it"), and uses a masculine singular instead. The person implicated in the action of the verb is shown by object suffixes. A corresponding English construction would be a prepositional phrase: "It's necessary for me." The word ይግባአኒ can be translated literally into Latin as *mihi oportet, it's necessary for me;* but in English it is usual to say "I must" or "I have to."

ደስ ኢሉኒ	*It pleased me.* lit *It says gladness to me.*
ደስ ኢሉና	*It pleased us.*
ይመስለኒ	*It seems to me.*
ይግባአኒ	*I must.* lit *It is fitting for me.*
ይአኽለኒ	*It is enough for me.*
ይሕሸኒ	*I am feeling better.* or *It's better for me.*
ይጥዕመኒ	*It's convenient for me.*
ይጠቅመኒ	*It is useful for me.*

These impersonal verbs are used in other tenses.

መሲሉኒ	*It seemed to me.*
ሓሽኒ	*I felt better.*
አኺሉኒ	*It was enough for me.*

Some other verbs are used either way, personal or impersonal, but in these verbs the personal form seems to predominate. Examples:

Impersonal	Personal	
የሕመኝ	ሐማመ	I am sick.
ጠምዩኝ	ጠምዩ	I am hungry.
ጸማኡኝ	ጸምኤ	I am thirsty.
ደክሙኝ	ደክመ	I am tired.
ተረዲኡኝ	ተረዲኤ	I understand.
ይከአለኝ	እኸእል	I can.

These other verbs, except the last, are gerundive in form, although they describe a present circumstance. To describe a circumstance in the past, add the appropriate form of the verb ነይሩ.

የሕመኝ ነይረ	ሐማመ ነይረ	I was sick.
የሕመዎ ነይሩ	ሐማሙ ነይሩ	He was sick.

LESSON 48

Stative Tenses

Like the English progressive tenses, stative tenses express a state of being. The Tigrinya verb is formed with the gerundive plus the appropriate form of ኣሎ or ነይሩ .

ኮፍ ኢለ ኣሎኹ።	*I am sitting.*
ኮፍ ኢለ ነይረ።	*I was sitting.*
ኮፍ ኢለ ሰራሐ።	*I worked while sitting.*
ሕጂ እቲ ቄልዓ ደቂሱ ኣሎ።	*The child is sleeping now.*
ሕጂ እቲ ቄልዓ ኮፍ ኢሉ ኣሎ።	*The child is sitting now.*
እቲ መንበር ተሰቢሩ ኣሎ።	*The chair is (still) broken.*
ጸጊበ ኣሎኹ።	*I'm satisfied; I'm full.*
ዐጊበ ኣሎኹ።	*I'm satisfied.*

When the action is in mind, rather than the resulting state of being, the ordinary tenses are used.

እታ መርከብ ምስ ትንቀሳቐስ ኮፍ እብል። *When the boat moves, I sit down.*

ጽባሕ ኣብ ልዕሊ ህድሞ ኮፍ ክብል ኢየ። *I'll sit on top of the hut tomorrow.*

LESSON 49

Conditionals

Conditional sentences can indicate possibility, impossibility, or improbability. The conditional clause comes before the principal clause.

A **possible** conditional clause is introduced by either
- (A) the simple imperfect and እንተኵን , or
- (B) እንተ and the simple perfect;
  እንተ and ዘ and the simple imperfect; or
  እንተ and the gerundive.

A **negative possible** conditional is introduced by
  ሃይ and the simple imperfect and እንተኵዐት ; or
  እንተዘይ and the simple perfect.

The principal clause will be in either the future or the imperative-jussive tense.

An **impossible** or **improbable** conditional clause is introduced by either
- (A) the gerundive and እንተ and ዘ and the simple imperfect of ኵን ; or
- (B) እንተ and ዘ and the simple imperfect; or
  እንተ and the simple perfect or the gerundive.

A **negative impossible** or **improbable** conditional is formed by
  እንተ and ዘይ and the simple imperfect or simple perfect.

The principal clause is formed with ም and the simple perfect, or for the negative አይ and ም and the simple perfect. To represent the action as completed, the appropriate form of ነይሩ is added to the simple perfect.

In the examples, the sentences continue from the left column over to the right, under the corresponding grammatical descriptions.

subordinate clauses	principal clauses

1. POSSIBLE CONDITIONS

1.(A) s–impf + እንተኾነ future
ትደልዮ እንተኾንካ፣ ውሰዶ።
If you like, *take it.*

future (colloquial) future
ክትጽሕፍ እንተኾንካ ርሳስ ክገዝአልካ እየ።
If you will write, *I'll buy you a pencil.*

NEGATIVE POSSIBLE CONDITIONS

ዘይ + s–impf + እንተኾነ future or imptv–juss
ዘይፈርህ እንተኾይኑ ምሳና ይኺድ።
If he isn't afraid, *let him go with us.*
ዘይመጽእ እንተኾይኑ አነ ክኸይድ እየ።
If he doesn't come, *I will go.*

1.(B) እንተ + s–pf future or imptv–juss
እቲ ፈረስ እንተተረኺበ ክሸጦ እየ።
If the horse is found, *I will sell it.*
ነቲ ፈረስ እንተረኺብካዮ ሳዕሪ አብልዓዮ።
If you find that horse, *feed him.*

እንተ + ዝ + s–impf + ኮይኑ future or imptv–juss
እንተ ዚኸይድ ኮይኑ ንገረኒ።
If he is going, *tell me.*

subordinate clauses	principal clauses

NEGATIVE POSSIBLE CONDITIONS (continued)

እንተ + gerundive	future or imptv–juss
እንተ በሊዕካዮ	ክትሓምም ኢኻ።
If you eat it,	*you will be sick.*

እንተዘይ + s–impf	future or imptv–juss
እንተዘይ መጻ	በይነይ ክኸይድ እየ።
If he does not come,	*I will go alone.*

2. **IMPOSSIBLE OR IMPROBABLE CONDITIONS**

2.(A) grndv + እንተ + ዘ + s–impf of ኮነ	ም + s–pf (+ ነይሩ)
ሓወይ መጺኡ እንተዚኸውን ·	ምተሓጕስኩ ነይረ።
If my brother had come,	*I would have been glad.*

2.(B) እንተ + ዘ + s–impf	ም + s–pf
እንተ ዝኸይድ	ዕረፍቲ ምረኸብኩ።
If he would go,	*I would find rest.*

እንተ + s–pf (or gerundive)	ም + s–pf
እንተጸሓፈ	አይምተሸገርኩን።
If he had written,	*I wouldn't be worried.*

NEGATIVE IMPOSSIBLE OR IMPROBABLE CONDITION

እንተ + ዘይ + s–impf or s–pf	ም + s–pf
ማይ እንተ ዘይሃርም	ትማሊ ምመጸ።
If it had not rained,	*he would've come yesterday.*

PART III

Common Expressions

These greetings and expressions can be used from the first days of study. There are both polite and familiar forms of address for speaking to both men and women. The familiar form of address is usually reserved for children, students, and young people. Unknown adults, adults older than oneself, and government officials regardless of age are spoken to with the polite form of address. When in doubt, the polite form is safe.

With few exceptions, the same verb form is used for "you" polite and "you" plural. The exceptions are found mainly in greetings and demonstratives. The pronoun "you" in the masculine polite singular is commonly used also for the masculine plural, although a specific plural form exists. The same is true for the pronoun "you" of the feminine polite singular and the feminine plural. The third person plural is often used as a polite form for the third person singular, e.g. መምህር መጺአም *The teacher has come.*

When speaking to or about groups of people that include both women and men, the masculine form is usual.

The following pages include greetings and other expressions which must be conjugated for person and number. Some examples are given to show what this typically involves, and others are left to the reader.

The abbreviations used are: s. *singular,* p. *plural,* pol. *polite,* m. *masculine,* f. *feminine,* c. *common.* The particle ዶ signifies a question. The traditional question mark consisting of three dots (፧) is written here, but the familiar mark (?) is displacing it.

A. Greetings

1. ሰላም — *Hello; good-bye* (lit. *peace*)

2. ደሓንዶ ሓዲርካ፧ — *Good morning* (lit. *Did you pass the night safely?* m.s. (addressing one man)
   ደሓንዶ ሓዲርኪ፧ — *Good morning* f.s. (addressing one woman)
   ደሓንዶ ሓዲርኩም፧ — m.pol. and m.p.
   ደሓንዶ ሓዲርክን፧ — f.pol. and f.p.
   ደሓንዶ ሓዲራትኩም፧ — m.polite, not commonly used
   ደሓንዶ ሓዲራትክን፧ — f.polite, not commonly used

3. ደሓንዶ ውዒልካ፧ — *Good afternoon* m.s.
   ደሓንዶ ውዒልኪ፧ — f.s.
   ደሓንዶ ውዒልኩም፧ — m.p. and m.pol.
   ደሓንዶ ውዒልክን፧ — f.p. and f.pol.

4. ደሓንዶ አምሲኻ፧ — *Good evening* m.s.
   ደሓንዶ አምሲኺ፧ — f.s.
   ደሓንዶ አምሲኹም፧ — m.p. and m.pol.
   ደሓንዶ አምሲኽን፧ — f.p. and f.pol.

5. ደሓን ውዓል — *Good-bye* (in the morning); *Have a nice day*
   ደሓን ውዓሊ — f.s.
   ደሓን ውዓሉ — m.p. and m.pol.
   ደሓን ውዓላ — f.p. and f.pol.

6. ደሓን አምሲ — *Good-bye* (in the afternoon) *Have a nice evening*
   ደሓን አምስዪ — f.s.
   ደሓን አምስዩ — m.p. and m.pol.
   ደሓን አምስያ — f.p. and f.pol.

7. ደሕን ሕደር Good night m.s.
    ደሕን ሕደሪ f.s.
    ደሕን ሕደሩ m.p. and m.pol.
    ደሕን ሕደራ f.p. and f.pol.

8. ደሕንዶ አሎኻ፧ Are you well? m.s.
    ከመይ አሎኻ፧ How are you? m.s.
    (አሎኻ is conjugated)

9. ደሕንዶ ቀኒኻ፧ How are you? (lit. How have you spent the week? This is used after a short time of not having seen someone.)

10. ይመስገን። ደሕንዶ አሎኹም፧ I am fine. How are you? (lit. May he (God) be thanked; are you well?)

11. እግዚአብሄር ይመስገን። Let God be thanked (this reply is given in response to every greeting that asks about one's well-being, before the same greeting is repeated)

    መስገን Thank him (God)
      abbrev. of ይመስገን
    መስገኖ Thanks to him (God)
      abbrev. of ይመስገኖ

12. ስድራኻ ደሕንዶ አለዉ፧ Is your family well?
    Are your parents well?

13. ይመስገን፤ ደሕን አለዉ። Thank you, they are well.

B. Courteous Expressions

14. የቾንየለይ — *Thank you* (lit, *May God give to you for me*)

15. ገንዘብካ — *You're welcome* (lit, *It is your possession.*)

16. ጽቡቕ — *Good, fine*

17. እወ — *Yes*

18. ሕራይ — *All right, OK*

19. አይፋለይን — *No* (m.s.; conjugated)

20. ይአክል — *It is enough*

21. አቤት — *Yes, sir* (when called)

22. በጃኻ — *Please* (conjugated)

23. ይቅሬታ — *I'm sorry; pardon me*
    ይቅረ በለለይ — *pardon me* m.s.
    ይቅረ በልለይ — *pardon me* f.s.
    ይቅረ በሉለይ — *pardon me* m.p.

24. አይትሕዘለይ — *Excuse me; forgive me* (conjugated; lit, *Don't hold it against me.*)

C. Expressions used in Visiting

25. መን እዩ ስምካ፧ — *What is your name?*

124

26.	ስመይ ዮሃንስ እዩ።	My name is John.
27.	ክንደይ ቆልዑ አለዉኻ፧	How many children do you have?
28.	ሓደ ቆልዓ አሎኒ። ሓንቲ ቆልዓ አላትኒ።	I have one child (boy). I have one child (girl).
29.	ክልተ ቆልዑ አለዉኒ።	I have two children.
30.	ቆልዑ የብለይን።	I don't have any children.
31.	ደቅኻ አበይ አለዉ፧	Where are your children?
32.	ደቀይ አብ ገዛ አለዉ።	My children are at home.
33.	ደቀይ ናብ ቤት ትምህርቲ ከይዶም።	My children went to school.
34.	ወደይ አብ ገዛ አሎ።	My son is at home.
35.	ክንደይ ዓመት ገይሩ፧ ክንደይ ዓመት ገይራ፧	How old is he? How old is she?
36.	ወዲ ክንደይ ዓመት እዩ፧ ጓል ክንደይ ዓመት እያ፧	How old is he? (polite) How old is she? (polite)
37.	ክንደይ ዓመት ጌርካ፧	How old are you?
38.	እዚአቶምዶ ደቅኻ እዮም፧	Are these your children?
39.	እወ ደቀይ እዮም።	Yes, they are my children.
40.	ደቀይ አይኮኑን።	They are not my children.
41.	እቲ ወደይ እዩ።	That boy is my son.

42.	እቲኣ፡ ጓል ጐረቤትና እያ።	That girl is our neighbor's daughter.
43.	ክንደይ ኣሕዋት ኣለዉኻ፧	How many brothers do you have?
44.	ምሉእ ዕድሜኻዶ ኣብ ኣስመራ ተቐሚጥካ፧	Have you lived in Asmara all your life?
45.	ገዛ ተኽለ ኣበይ እዩ፧ እንዳ ተኽለ ገዛ ኣበይ እዩ፧	Where does Tekle live?
46.	እቶ፡ ኩፍ በል እተዊ፡ ኩፍ በሊ እተዉ፡ ኩፍ በሉ እተዋ፡ ኩፍ በላ	Come in; sit down. m.s. f.s. m.pl. or m.pol. f.pl. or f.pol.
47.	ጣይታዶ ትበልዕ ኢኻ፧	Do you eat taita (a kind of bread)?
48.	እወ፡ ጣይታ እበልዕ እየ።	Yes, I eat taita.
49.	ብላዕ ብልዒ ብልዑ ብላ፞ዓ	Eat. m.s. (used at table) f.s. m.pl. or m.pol. f.pl. or f.pol.
50.	እበልዕ ኣሎኹ	I am eating.
51.	ጸጊበ	I'm satisfied. (food only)
52.	ሻሂ'ዶ ትሰቲ ኢኻ፧	Do you drink tea?
53.	እወ፡ ሻሂ እሰቲ እየ።	Yes, I drink tea.
54.	እቲ ማይ ፈሊሑ'ዶ፧	Has the water boiled?

55.	ሻሂ አፍልሒ።	Boil the tea.
56.	ሻሂ ክነፍልሐልኩም።	We will make tea for you.
57.	ጡዑም	Very good! Delicious! (should always be said)
58.	ጡዑም ይሃብኩም።	Thank you (the reply to ጡዑም; lit. May he (God) give you good things.
59.	ከጥዕም'ዶ ተፍቅደለይ፧	May I taste it?
60.	እዚ ንምንታይ ይጠቅም፧	What is this useful for?
61.	መጎጎ ንመስንክቲ ይጠቅም።	The magogo is used for baking.
62.	ከመይ ከም ዚግበር አርእየኒ።	Show me how to do it.
63.	ገዛና ቀረባ እዩ።	Our house is nearby.
64.	ጎረባብቲ ኢና።	We are neighbors.
65.	ገዛኻ ቀረባ'ዶ እዩ፧	Is your house near?
66.	ገዛይ ርሑቕ እዩ።	My house is far.
67.	ክኸይድ ፍቓድካ'ዶ እዩ፧	May I go?
68.	ካልእ ምዓልቲ ከመጽእ እየ።	I'll come another time.
69.	ዓርቢ'ዶ ናብ ገዛና ክትመጽእ ይጥዕመካ፧	Would Friday be convenient for you to come to our house?

70.	ሎሚ ክመጽእ አይጥዕመንን እዩ።	It is not convenient for me to come today.
71.	ጽባሕ ክመጽእ ይጥዕመኒ እዩ።	It is convenient for me to come tomorrow
	ጽባሕ ክኸይድ ይጥዕመኒ እዩ።	It is convenient for me to go tomorrow
72.	ሕጂ ናብ ገዛይ ክምለስ እየ።	I will return to my house now.
73.	ትማሊ'ዶ ናብ ገለ ገዛ ኬድካ፧	Did you go to any house yesterday?
74.	ምስ መን ኬድካ፧	Whom did you go with?
75.	ምስ ዓርከይ ከይደ።	I went with my friend.
76.	አብቲ ገዛ እንታይ ጌርካ፧	What did you do in the house?
77.	ምስቶም ሰብ ተላሊና።	We became acquainted with those people.
78.	ተረዲኡካ'ዶ፧	Do you understand?
79.	ተረዲኡኒ	I understand. (not conjugated)
	አስተውዒለ	I understand.
80.	አይተረድአንን	I don't understand. We don't understand.
81.	ትግርኛ'ዶ ትዛረብ ኢኻ፧	Do you speak Tigrinya?
82.	ትግርኛ ብዙሕ አይዛረብን እየ።	I don't speak much Tigrinya.

83.	ትግርኛ ከመሃር እደሊ አሎኹ።	I want to learn Tigrinya.
84.	እንግሊዝ እዛረብ እየ።	I speak English.
85.	እንግሊዝ ከመሃር አይደልን እየ።	I don't want to learn English.
86.	እንታይ ትብል አሎኻ፤ ድገሞ፤	What are you saying? Repeat it.
87.	ቀስ በል።	Do it slowly.
88.	ቀስ ኢልካ ተዛረብ።	Speak slowly.
89.	እዚ እንታይ ይበሃል፤	What is this called?
90.	ልክዕ ድዩ፤	Is it correct?
91.	አንቢብካ'ዶ ትኽእል፤	Can you read?
92.	አንቢብ አይክእልን እየ።	I cannot read.
93.	እንግሊዝ ከንብብ እኽእል እየ።	I can read English.
94.	ከንብበልካ'ዶ፤	Shall I read to you?
95.	ረሲዔዮ። ድሓሪ ሕጂ ግና ከዝክሮ እየ።	I forgot it, but after this I will remember it.
96.	መአስ መጺአካ፤	When did you come?
97.	ቅድሚ ሰለስተ ሰሙን መጺኤ።	I came three weeks ago.
98.	ቅድሚ ክልተ ወርሒ መጽኤ።	I came two months ago.

99.	ዓድና ይሰማምዓኩም'ዶ ኣሎ፤	Do you like our country?
100.	ካብ አየናይ ሃገር መጺእካ፤	What country did you come from?
101.	ካብ አሜሪካ መጺኤ።	I came from America.
102.	ብባሕሪ መጺኤ።	I came by sea.
103.	ብነፋሪት መጺኤ።	I came by plane.
104.	ብሰለስተ ሰሙን ኣቲና።	It took three weeks for us to come.
105.	ተመርዒኻ'ዶ፤	Are you married?
106.	እወ፡ ተመርዐየ፤	Yes, I am married.
107.	አይተመርዓኹን።	I am not married.
108.	እንታይ እዩ ስራሕካ፤	What is your work?
109.	መምህር እየ።	I'm a teacher.
110.	ኣላይት ሕሙማት እየ።	I'm a nurse.
111.	ቃል እግዚኣብሄር ክነግር መጺኤ።	I came to tell God's word.
112.	አቦይ ምዉት እየ።	My father is dead.
113.	ትማሊ	Yesterday.
114.	ሎሚ ንግሆ	This morning.
115.	ሎሚ ምሸት	This evening.

116.	ተጠንቀቕ	Be careful.
117.	ቀልጥፍ	Hurry up.
118.	ማኪና ደው ኣብላ።	Stop the car.
119.	ግደፍ	Leave it! Stop!
120.	ኣይትሓዞ	Don't take hold of it! Don't touch.
121.	ፈንዎ	Let it go. (an animal or moving object) m.s.
	ፈንዋ	Let it go. f.s.
122.	ስማዕ	Listen!
123.	ትሃዊኽ ኣሎኹ።	I'm in a hurry.
124.	በበይኑ እዩ	It's different. It's not the same.
125.	ምለሶ	Put it back.
126.	ኣቐምጠ	Put it down.
127.	ኣይተፈልጠን	It is not known.
128.	ተሰከመለይ ግዳ።	Carry this for me, please.
129.	ክሕግዘካ'ዶ፧	May I help you?
130.	በጃኻ ሓግዘኒ	Please help me.
131.	ካብ ኣሥመራ መኣስ ክትከይድ ኢኻ፧	When will you leave from Asmara?

132.	ድሕሪ ሹዱሽተ ወርሒ ክኸይድ እየ።	I will leave in six months.
133.	ናበይ ትኸይድ ኣሎኻ፧	Where are you going?
134.	ክንደይ ወርሒ ክትጸንሕ ኢኻ፧	How many months will you stay?
135.	ተማላኣኒ	Give me a ride.
136.	ስፍራ የልቦን።	There is no room.
137.	ልማድና አይኮነን	It isn't our custom.
138.	እዚ ምግባር ሕማቕ እዩ።	To do this is bad.
139.	ስራሕ'ዶ ሒዝካ፧	Are you busy? (lit. Is your work keeping you?)
140.	ጠምየ ጠምየን ጠምዮም	I am hungry. She is hungry. f.pol. They are hungry. m.p. or m.pol.
141.	ጠሚኻ'ዶ፧	Are you hungry?
142.	ጸሚእካ'ዶ፧	Are you thirsty?
143.	ጸሚኤ። ጸሚኡ።	I am thirsty. He is thirsty.
144.	ሐሚምካ ዲኻ፧ ሐሚምኪ ዲኺ፧	Are you sick? m.s. Are you sick? f.s.
145.	ሐሚመ	I am sick.
146.	ጉንፋዕ ሒዙኒ።	I have a cold.

147.	ይሕሽኒ	I am better.
148.	ተጸሊእዎ	He is a little sick.
149.	ሓዊኻ'ዶ፤	Are you better?
150.	ደኺምካ ዲኻ፤	Are you tired? m.s.
	ደኺምኪ ዲኺ፤	Are you tired? f.s.
151.	ደኺመ	I am tired.
152.	ቆሪሩ	I am cold.
153.	ሎሚ ሃሩር አሎ።	It is hot today.
154.	ሎሚ ቍሪ አሎ።	It is cold today.
155.	ተሓጒሰ	I'm glad
156.	አብዩ	He refused.
	አብያ	She refused.
	አብዮም	They refused. m.p.
	አብየን	They refused. f.p.
157.	ይመስለኒ።	It seems to me.
158.	"ሕራይ" ኢሉ።	He said "OK."
159.	ሕጂ ኺድ እሞ፤	Go now, and return tomorrow.
	ጽባሕ ተመለስ።	(addressed to m.s.)
160.	ደሓር ግበሮ።	Do it later. m.s.
	ደሓር ግበርዮ።	Do it later. f.s.
161.	ደሓር ይሕሽኒ።	Later is better for me.
162.	ሓደሓደ ግዜ	Sometimes.

163.	ኩሉ ሳዕ	*Always.*
164.	ሓደ ጥራይ አሎ።	*There is only one.*
165.	ግዜ የብለይን።	*I don't have time.*
166.	ተስፋ እገብር። ተስፋ አሎኒ።	*I'm hopeful., I hope so.*
167.	ክርእዮ'ዶ፧	*May I see it?*
168.	ምስ'ቲ ሰብ አፋልጠኒ።	*Introduce me to that person.*
169.	ክስእለካ'ዶ፧ ክስእለኪ'ዶ፧	*May I take your picture?* m.s. *May I take your picture?* f.s.
170.	ናብ ዓደይ ክሰደ ደልየ።	*I want to send it to my country.*
171.	እብዚ ውሽጢ መካበብያ፡ ክንደይ ስድራ አለዉ፧	*How many families live together in this compound?*
172.	ክልተ ስድራ አለዉ።	*There are two families.*
173.	መገዲ አዲስ አበባ ክንደይ መዓልቲ የኸይድ፧	*How many days does it take to go to Addis Ababa?*
174.	ዓድኻ ብእግሪ ክንደይ ሰዓት የኸይድ፧	*How many hours does it take to go to your village by foot?*
175.	መዓስ ክትበጽሓና ኢኻ፧	*When will you visit us?*
176.	ሰንበት ክበጽሓኩም እየ።	*Sunday I will visit you.*

C. Household Expressions

177. ሙዑይ ማይ አምጽእ። Bring hot water.

178. ዝሑል ማይ አምጽእ። Bring cold water.

179. ነቲ ቒልዓ ምስ ተንስኤ አምጽእዮ። Bring the lad when he wakes up. (addressed to f.s.)

180. ምስ ተንስኤት ጸውዕኒ። When she wakes up, call me.

181. ነቲ ሕጻን ሕጸብዮ። Wash the baby.

182. እግሪ'ዶ ተኺላ፧ Can she walk?

183. ክዳን ቀይርሉ። Change the [child's] clothes.

184. ክዳውንቲ ሕጸብዮ። Wash the clothes.
     ክዳውንቲ ስጥሕዮ። Let the clothes air dry.

185. ክዳውንቲ አስታርር። Iron the clothes. m.s.
     ክዳውንቲ አስታርሪ። f.s.
     ክዳውንቲ አስታርሩ። m.p.
     ክዳውንቲ አስታርራ። f.p.

186. ማይ ስኸትቲ። Put the water on the fire. (the verb is only for liquids)

187. እቲ ማይ አውርዲዮ ካብ እቶን። Take the water off the fire.

188. ድንሽ አብስሊ። Cook the potatoes. (f.s.)

189. ሰደቓ አዳልዊ። Set the table. (m.s.)

190. ሽሐውንቲ ሕጸቢ። Wash the dishes. (f.s.)

191.	ገዛ አጽርዮ።	Clean the house. (m.s.)
192.	ምድሪ ቤት ኮስትር።	Sweep the floor. (m.s.)
193.	ምድሪ ቤት ወልውሊ።	Wash the floor. (f.s.)
194.	ነቲ መናብር ንገፎ።	Dust the chairs. (m.s.)
195.	ወልዓዮ or ኣብርሃዮ።	Turn on [the light]. (m.s.)
196.	እጎድዮ or ሓዊ እጎዲ።	Light the fire. (f.s.)
197.	ኣጥፍኣዮ።	Turn off [light or fire]. (m.s.)
198.	ማይ ዕጸዎ።	Turn off the water. (m.s.)
199.	ማይ ክፈትዮ።	Turn on the water. (f.s.)
200.	ብምንታይ ተሰርሑ፧	How is it made?
201.	ባዕልኻ'ዶ ሰሪሕካዮ።	Have you made it yourself?
202.	ክዳውንተይ ብማኪና እዮ ተሰፍዩ።	My clothes are sewn by machine.
203.	እንታይ ኣብሊዖምኹም፧	What did they give you to eat?
204.	ዝግኒ ኣብሊዖሙና።	They gave us zigeni.
205.	ሻሂ ኣስትዮሙና።	They gave us tea.
206.	እንታይ ዓይነት ጸብሒ ቀሪቦሙልካ፧	What kind of sauce did they prepare for you?
207.	ሽሮ ቀሪቦሙለይ።	They prepared shiro for me.

E. At the Market

208. እኽሊ አበይ እዩ ዝሽየጥ፧ — *Where is grain sold?*

209. እቲ እንታይ ዕይነት እኽሊ እዩ፧ — *What kind of grain is that?*

210. አብ ክረምቲ ክንደይ ወርሒ አሎ፧ — *How many months is the rainy season?*

211. ክርቢት ግዛእለይ። — *Buy matches for me.*

212. ጽባሕ ክኸፍለካ እየ። — *I will pay you tomorrow.*

F. In the School

213. ስቕ በል or ትም በል። — *Be quiet.*

214. ደው በል። — *Stand up.*

215. አብ ሰሌዳ ጽሓፍ። — *Write on the chalkboard.*

216. ሰሌዳ ወልውል። — *Clean the chalkboard.*

217. አቃጭላ። — *Ring it [the bell].*

218. ርሳሰይ'ዶ ክጽርብ፧ — *May I sharpen my pencil?*

219. ተመሃሮ አብ ቤት ትምህርቲ ይመሃሩ። — *The students learn in the school.*

220. ሰዓት ዐሰርተው ሓደን ርብዕን ትምህርቲ አሎና። — *At eleven-fifteen we have class.*

221. መን ምሂሩካ፧ — *Who taught you?*

222.	አቶ ገብረሂወት ምሂሩኒ።	Ato Gebre-Hiwet taught me.
223.	አበይ ተማሂርካ፤	Where did you go to school?
224.	አብ አየናይ ክፍሊ ትምህር አሎኻ፤	What grade are you in?
225.	ታስዓይ ክፍሊ ምስ ወዳእኩ መምህር ክኸውን እየ።	When I finish ninth grade, I'll become a teacher.
226.	ንጸሊ።	Let us pray.
227.	ነዚ ጥቅሲ እጽንዓዮ።	Memorize (m.s.) this verse.
228.	አየናይ መዝሙር ክንዝምር፤	Which song shall we sing?

G. At Clinic

229.	እንታይ የሕመካ፤	What's wrong with you?
230.	መአስ ጀሚሩካ፤	When did it begin?
231.	አበይ የቕንዘወካ፤	Where do you have pain?
232.	ረስኒ'ዶ አሎካ፤	Do you have a fever?
233.	የውጽእካ'ዶ፤	Do you have diarrhea?
234.	የምልሰካ'ዶ፤	Do you have vomiting?

H. Greetings for Special Occasions

235. ርሑስ በዓል ፋሲካ ይግበርልካ፡፡ Happy Easter! (conjugated)

236. ርሑስ በዓል ልደት ይግበርልካ፡፡ Merry Christmas! (conjugated)

237. ርሑስ አውደ ዓመት ይግበርልካ፡፡ Happy New Year! (conjugated)

238. አሕቢሩ፡፡ The same to you. lit *Be united in this wish.* (Reply to nos. 235, 236, and 237)

239. እግዚአብሄር ይምሐርካ፡፡ Get well soon. lit *May God have mercy on you.*

240. ምሕረት የውርደልካ፡፡ Get well soon. lit *May mercy descend on you.*

241. እግዚአብሄር የጽንዕካ May God strengthen you (to someone in mourning; sg.).
or እግዚአብሄር የበርትዕካ

or እግዚአብሄር ጽንዓት ይሃብኩም፡፡ (the same, pl.)

242. አይትሕሰሙ፡፡ (Reply to no. 241. lit *May you not find evil.*)
or ሕሰም አይትርከቡ፡፡

243. መገዲ ደሕን ይውስድካ፡፡ Have a good trip. (m.s.) (can be conjugated)

244. ብደሕን እቶ፡፡ Bon voyage.

245. እንቋዕ ብደሕን መጻእካ፡፡ Welcome. lit *Wonderful that you have arrived safely.*

246. እንቋዕ ብድሓን ጸናሕካ። Glad to see you. (Reply to no. 245. lit *Wonderful that you have stayed well.*)

247. እግዚአብሄር የዕብዮ። *May God make him grow* (to parents of a newborn or at baptism).

248. አሜን። *Amen.* This is used to reply to all expressions of good will.